ᴍᴇ FOR HEROES

6c 95

A Time for Heroes

Brother Andrew
with
Dave and Neta Jackson

VINE
BOOKS

Servant Publications
Ann Arbor, Michigan

Copyright © 1988 by Open Doors International
All rights reserved.

Vine Books is an imprint of Servant Publications especially
designed to serve Evangelical Christians.

Published by Servant Books
P.O. Box 8617
Ann Arbor, Michigan 48107

Scripture quotations, unless otherwise noted, are from the
Holy Bible Revised Standard Version, © 1972 by Thomas Nelson
Inc.

Cover design by Michael Andaloro
Cover illustration by Kevin Davidson

Dutch-born Brother Andrew is founder and international
president of Open Doors with Brother Andrew, a world-wide
mission organization supporting persecuted and threatened
Christians in Eastern Europe, China, Africa, Latin America
and the Middle East.

Printed in the United States of America
ISBN 0-89283-395-5
88 89 90 91 92 10 9 8 7 6 5 4 3 2 1

Library of Congress Cataloging-in-Publication Data

Andrew, Brother.
   A time for heroes / Brother Andrew with Dave and Neta
Jackson.
      p. cm.
      ISBN 0-89283-395-5
   1. Bible—Biography. 2. Christian life—1960-. I. Jackson,
Dave. II. Jackson, Neta. III. Title.
BS571.A65   1988
220.9'2   88-6532
                                                    CIP

And all these,
though well attested by their faith,
did not receive what was promised
since God had foreseen
something better for us,
that apart from us
they should not be made perfect.
(Heb 11:39, 40)

Table of Contents

Introduction

THROUGHOUT OUR WORLD men and women have influenced entire generations by obeying God and turning vision into action. What conditions are necessary to be used by God? How can a generation be changed? When is it necessary to resist godless civil authority? This study of the heroes of the faith addresses these and many other questions.

"God's smuggler" is what many have called me because for over thirty years I have dedicated myself to getting the Scriptures into the hands of the suffering church and giving hope to persecuted Christians around the world. In the process I have come to know many modern heroes of the faith who exemplify the biblical heroes discussed in this book.

Hebrews 11 is the great "Hall of Faith" in the Bible, where the people who by faith gave their lives for the faith are honored throughout the church. It lists people God used mightily, and it lists people whom God rescued from the gutter, so to speak—people like a slave baby floating on a river and a coward withering in the stomach of a whale.

But does God still want heroes of the faith today? As we read the Bible, we can recognize many similarities between the conditions in Bible times and those of today. There was and continues to be a tremendous spiritual battle going on in the world. If there weren't, there would be no need for heroes of the faith. In fact, there would be no need for faith. But the spiritual conflict has not lessened. Many rightly say that it has intensified.

When we continue to study God's Word, we see how God stepped into situations of old by calling a man or a woman or a nation, and we see that whatever God did in that instance to change the world, he is likely to do again today because he is always true to his own character and to his own unfailing Word. If the battle has heated up, so has the need for heroes of the faith.

It could be that God is calling you; consider the possibility as you study *A Time for Heroes*. This book has impressed upon my heart the fact that most heroes of the faith in the Bible became martyrs. One big problem in *our* time is that our heroes of the faith are celebrities. Never make *me* a celebrity . . . please.

Brother Andrew

ONE

Job: Foundations That Endure Calamity

A MISSIONARY FRIEND OF MINE spent years in a prison in China because he would not deny his Lord and would not flee when the communists took over. His possessions were stripped away, and the mental torture he endured brought him to the point where he couldn't even form coherent thoughts.

"Lord," he cried, "my whole being craves to worship you, yet my mind is so confused that I can't even pray. If I stand in my cell, will you accept that as an act of worship?"

Even though his mind wouldn't function, he won the spiritual battle because he refused to doubt the character of God. He was absolutely invincible in the Lord.

Not many of us have had to endure the physical stress and mental torture of a prison cell or of being persecuted for our faith. But how many of us begin to doubt God's love, complain about our situation, feel sorry for ourselves, or otherwise waver in our faith when we experience the stresses of life that are our common lot?

This is not to say that the crises we face are not real ones. The loss of a job, the death of a child, a serious accident or illness can happen to any one of us—and maybe already has—and can test the faith and endurance of even the stoutest heart. But our response in these times of calamity is not born overnight; rather, it is built over time in the way we face little disappointments, loss, sickness, frustration, rejection, pain.

Our society is quick to make heroes of media personalities—and just as quick to cut them down. Like children playing "He-man" and "She-ra," we want instant solutions to our problems—and when they are not forthcoming, we blame the latest heroes we have created and toss them out.

But underneath, the world today is hungry for real heroes—people whose lives are built on a solid foundation, who do not waver when the going gets tough, who will stand by another in his time of weakness and say, "Have courage; God *is* faithful. I've been there, too." These heroes of faith, however, do not appear in a flash of light, like cartoon heroes; they grow through facing the small adversities of life with eyes of faith.

In times of illness, anxiety, persecution, or sorrow, the Bible explains that _how we cope_ depends on _what we know_ about God. In Hebrews 11:1, faith is defined as "the assurance of things hoped for, the conviction of things not seen." In other words, faith consists of our inner knowledge of the supernatural and the unseen, by means of which we can endure and continue in spite of difficult circumstances.

Throughout the Bible we see how God took hold of men or women during a time of crisis—whether personal or national—and made them heroes of the faith. Their struggles were written down for our benefit to help us discover the true character of God. Romans 4:23-24 says, "But the words . . . were written not for [Abraham's] sake alone, but for ours also."

One of the most dramatic accounts in Scripture of coping with crises is the story of Job. He exceeded all the other Bible heroes in the amount and suddenness of calamity that befell him. Here was a wealthy man, honest in all his dealings, the most respected man in the community. He was a godly man, with an enviable family of ten privileged children (though they were somewhat spoiled, with a weakness for food and festivities), for whom he expressed a great deal of ongoing spiritual concern and love.

And then suddenly, Job's entire empire was wiped out. His flocks and herds were raided by robber bands, and his servants were killed. A great fire wiped out what wealth was left by the bandits. But as if that were not enough, all his sons and daughters were crushed to death when a fierce wind caused the house they were in to collapse. Finally, he developed painful boils all over his body, from his scalp to the soles of his feet.

The most astonishing thing about this story, however, is that it appears that *God allowed these calamities to happen to Job* as a test of his faithfulness and a witness to Satan!

It is human nature to question suffering, and though the Book of Job answers quite a few of those questions, it raises still others. One question that is never answered in the biblical account of Job's story is why his life was chosen as a battleground between God and Satan. Job struggled deeply with this question and others related to his great suffering. "Why me?" he cried out to God. "Why was I ever born?"

Though Job was baffled by this mystery, he did not let it destroy his faith. He allowed his suffering to refine his character so he could fight despair and cling to hope. Through it all, Job insisted on his righteousness before God, and he never once doubted the character of God.

The Prevalence of Doubt

Doubt is a basic part of the human personality. We have been created with a free will which allows us to question, to doubt, to discover for ourselves. Even as Christians, we occasionally doubt God's Word—whether God has really said something or not. I firmly believe that God accepts our doubts. But one thing he won't accept is doubts about his character. For that reason, the time we spend studying God's Word should be devoted primarily to discovering his character. It's interesting to study prophecy, but our interpretations may be in error. It's interesting to work on deciphering the difficult doctrinal teachings of the Word, but again, we may make a mistake. A time may come when all those theories go up for grabs and everything we hold dear is taken away from us—our liberty, our Bible, our church—but no one can take away our fundamental trust in God and our understanding of who he is.

Job was a man who lost everything. He was even left all alone by his so-called friends as soon as his fortunes turned sour. "Job must be a terrible sinner," they reasoned, "or else all this suffering would not have come upon him." But Job was also a man who knew God. Even his great loss, his overwhelming sorrow, his agonizing pain could not shake his fundamental trust in who God is.

What Job Knew about God

At the height of the satanic attacks against Job, his friend Eliphaz said, "What do you know that we do not know? What do you understand that is not clear to us?" (Jb 15:9). Although meant sarcastically, these questions were the turning point in the discourse. If we are sure of our salvation in Jesus Christ and sure of our way with God, people who don't share this certainty will always attack and mock us.

But what *did* Job know about God that his accusers didn't know?

1. He Knew God Was There

Seeing how devoted Job was to his family, the enemy hit hard at that very spot. Surely, Satan speculated, the loss of his family will alienate him from God. So Satan killed all of Job's children. After that, the loss of Job's wealth was probably incidental. But these disasters did not cause Job to curse God or to doubt his existence. After Satan's attacks, "Then Job arose, and rent his robe, and shaved his head, and fell upon the ground, and worshiped. And he said, 'Naked I came from my mother's womb, and naked shall I return; the Lord gave, and the Lord has taken away; blessed be the name of the Lord'" (Jb 1:20-22).

In all this Job did not sin or charge God with wrong.

How could he *worship* in the context of such great anguish? This is very difficult for us to understand. But in spite of being a supremely devoted family man, the ultimate meaning in Job's life had never been centered on his family or his wealth. Had it been, he probably would have been destroyed, as Satan anticipated. Instead, God had been the central focus for Job. God was still there, and that was enough for Job to hold onto.

In spite of his great anguish of heart, Job *worshiped* the Lord and declared (as he did throughout the whole discourse with his friends) his certainty that God was there. He did not allow the disasters, his pain, or his inability to understand what was happening to him to unravel his certainty of God's existence.

2. He Knew God Was Righteous

Job was also strengthened by his vision of God's righteousness and his own family's need for forgiveness. Because of his awareness, he knew how to protect his family from condemnation. In fact, Job regularly prepared a sacrifice to the Lord, saying: "It may be that my sons have sinned, and cursed God in their hearts" (Jb 1:5). This was a remarkable act, especially since his children were already grown. What a father he must have been!

I have five children, and occasionally I'll manage to get

them all together for a time of prayer and worship, but not very regularly. They are busy with their own lives and affairs. But Job was scrupulous about praying for his children, sacrificing a burnt offering for each one in case they had fallen away from God.

Sometimes we have an exaggerated idea of what it takes to be a hero of the faith—crossing dangerous borders, preaching to large crowds, winning whole nations for Christ. No, faithfulness begins at home. A hero is a father or mother who has children sanctified by the blood of the Lamb, meeting together with them at the cross!

3. He Knew God Accepted Him

There is a scene in chapter two of the Book of Job that I cannot fully explain. It took place in Heaven, with the angels and even the devil in attendance at God's throne. "Have you seen my servant Job?" God asked Satan. "He is blameless and upright." Later, Job's friends questioned whether Job could possibly be upright (Jb 8:6), not knowing that God had already declared that he was so.

How can anyone, stained every day by sin, possibly be blameless before God? By the blood of an atoning sacrifice. God shuns evil; Job knew this, so he submitted to regular cleansing, offering the sacrifices that looked forward to the fulfilling sacrifice of Jesus, the Lamb of God. Before the hosts of Heaven, Job was declared to be unique in all the earth in maintaining his integrity. In other words, God said, "I'm proud of him." This was not because Job was sinless, but because he was forgiven and covered by God's righteousness.

Job knew this, too. He knew he was a sinful man, but he had kept his accounts straight with God. Even in the midst of his terrible troubles, Job was able to rest securely in God's acceptance of him.

Isn't it a good feeling to know that right now, because of the atoning sacrifice of Jesus on the cross, God is proud of you? You and I have no righteousness in ourselves. But no matter how many fingers point at us, no matter how many storms try to beat us down, *we are accepted by God,* our sins covered by the blood of Jesus. Really taken to heart, wouldn't that make anybody a hero of the faith?

Faith: The Answer to Fear

However, there was one weak point in Job's life, one I hesitate to mention because it was so personal. But Job himself confessed that "the thing which I greatly feared is come upon me, and that which I was afraid of is come unto me" (Jb 3:25 KJV). Fear and faith can never be friends, and in the measure that God fills our hearts with faith, fear has to go. The same is true of love, which drives out hatred and doubt. Unfortunately, the reverse is also true: if we let fear rule our hearts, it chokes out faith.

Somewhere in all his uprightness, Job had a secret fear. It had lingered deep within his consciousness, gnawing away at his security in life. "Maybe I won't have all this forever," he thought. "Maybe these gifts of God—my beautiful family, my prosperity, my health, my standing in the community—will be taken from me. Will I be strong then? Will I be able to bear it?"

Do you know why I hesitate to be so personal? Because I had a great friend in the Lord, Corrie ten Boom, with whom I worked for twenty-five years. She was a courageous servant of God, a true heroine of the faith admired by millions through her books and films. Yet she said, "I have one fear: that I will have a stroke and won't be able to communicate any longer. I'll have to spend years in my bed like a vegetable, coming to an end the same way my mother did."

That was the only fear I ever saw in Corrie, and that was exactly what happened to her.

Faith is the only answer to fear, and it must permeate

every corner of our lives, including the way we are going to end this life. When we are full of faith, we can just shout at the devil that there's nothing to be afraid of. There wasn't anything to fear in Job's life, either, because as the devil quickly pointed out, God had put a protective hedge of blessing around him, just as he does around us.

How could the removing of that hedge be explained to Job? It couldn't, yet more than knowing some *thing,* Job knew some *One.* No matter what his friends (and his wife) said against him, Job declared that "I have not denied the words of the Holy One" (Jb 6:10).

Millions of people today in countries where suffering is great have not denied the faithfulness of God, despite intense persecution for their belief. In the pressure cooker, you really come to know the One who loves you infinitely.

It Helps to Know What the End Will Be

What else did Job know that the others didn't? In Job 19:25, he proclaimed, "I know that my Redeemer lives." He believed with all his heart in God's redemption, and he repeated his faith in the resurrection three times: "Yet in my flesh I will see God; I myself will see him with my own eyes—I, and not another" (19:26b, 27 NIV).

Because of *what he knew* and the *One he knew,* Job could cope with all the suffering. Another life was to follow, one where no enemy could intrude and no one could take away his joy. With a ringing proclamation of faith, he declared, "But he knows the way that I take; when he has tested me, I will come forth as gold" (Jb 23:10 NIV).

What a tremendous message! Job recognized that God does test us, and he repeated the truth of what God had already declared—that Job was righteous. That was his testimony, as it should be ours. God says, "You are righteous in Christ," and we should respond, "Yes, I am righteous because God declares it."

That's what the word "testimony" is all about: repeating what God has already said about me. Once I was a sinner, but the moment I admit it and seek forgiveness, asking Jesus to come into my heart and life, then I am no longer counted a sinner. From that moment on I am seen by God as righteousness, and God will treat me as such.

When Job's friends asked repeatedly, "How can a man be righteous?" they were attempting to undermine the very basis of his faith. So Job returned again and again to the fact that he was righteous because of the sacrifice he believed in. The blood was shed for the remission of sins—Job's included.

The Rewards of Faith

What was the final result when Job replaced his secret fear with an open declaration of faith? At the beginning of the story, he had seven sons and three daughters, along with 7,000 sheep, 3,000 camels, 500 yoke of oxen, and 500 donkeys. He lost them all, without letting a single word of sin pass his lips. Afterward, God again blessed him with seven sons and three daughters, plus 14,000 sheep, 6,000 camels, 1,000 yoke of oxen, and 1,000 donkeys—double the wealth with which he had started (see Job 42). And Job lived a good, long life to enjoy his children's children, even to great-great grandchildren.

Yes, God also gave him double the number of his children; the first ten were in Heaven, and Job knew it. You can take the silence of this verse as God's approval of Job's faith in the glorious resurrection. Can anyone be so rich as believing Christian parents?

Was the suffering worth it? We won't be able to understand the full implications of those events until we reach Heaven, but think about this: the date of the Book of Job is unknown, but the context is patriarchal, possibly reflecting the time of Abraham. Consider these two great men of God. Suppose that in response to Job's faithfulness under trial, God was touched and made a commitment to be more intimate with those who trusted in him. Could this be behind his saying, "Shall I hide from Abraham what I am about to do?" (Gn 18:17).

God puts tremendous trust in his heroes of the faith, enabling them to change the course of history not only on earth but also in heavenly realms. He places so much confidence in us that he gives us his Word and the responsibility to carry that Word, preach it, and most of all, live it before all the world, so others can come to know the God who is righteousness.

Job has walked before us, a hero of the faith for today. His example stands beside us in our time of suffering, doubt, and struggle, saying, "Have courage; God *is* faithful. I've been there, too." Job has shown us that no matter what losses we face, even when all else fails us, God is there. And God has provided a way for us to stand before him, just as Job did, forgiven and fully accepted. We too can know that because of God's redemption and the resurrection of Jesus, what may seem like the end of all earth's pleasures and treasures is not the end at all.

Truly believing this will provide the answer to all our fears. Like Job, we too can be a hero of the faith, pointing the way to the true foundation for happiness and security: a relationship with God the Father and his Son Jesus Christ.

TWO

Moses: A Hero to Stand in the Gap

I N JULY 1987, A GREAT MAN of God died at the age of eighty-nine. He was Peter Deyneka, Sr., the founder of the Slavic Gospel Association (SGA). He emigrated from Russia to the United States in 1914 and has been known ever since for his work on behalf of Christians living in Eastern Europe and the Soviet Union.

Many Russians who have left their country never looked back to the land from which they came. But not Peter Deyneka. He remained standing in the gap, and therein lies his greatness.

The image of a hero standing in the gap refers to someone who could move on to a life of ease, comfort, and safety, but who instead chooses to remain in a place of hardship and in some cases danger in order to help others. Peter was certainly such a person.

Millions of believers from behind the Iron Curtain have reason to thank God for Peter's influence which still lives through his children, the mission he founded (SGA), the Russian Bible School, numerous broadcasts, books, and presentations to other Christians to arouse their interest and prayer on behalf of the church in the Soviet Union.

This is what it means to be a hero standing in the gap.

Why Make the Sacrifice?

Some Christians think that the most important thing in life is to be sure that they go to Heaven when they die. But if that is so, why did two of the greatest men in the Bible—Moses in the Old Testament and the apostle Paul in the New Testament—both clearly express their willingness to be blotted out from the Book of Life? What could possibly be more important than having a guaranteed place in Heaven?

These two heroes of the faith believed that there was indeed something more important. Let's explore this further by looking at an event in the life of Moses.

The story is found in Exodus 32. Moses had been up on Mount Sinai for several days receiving God's Law, but while he was gone the people got impatient and decided to make an idol—a golden calf—and they worshiped it. Then this is what happened:

> And the Lord said to Moses, "Go down; for your people, whom you brought up out of the land of Egypt, have corrupted themselves; they have turned aside quickly out of the way which I commanded them. . . . I have seen this people, and behold, it is a stiff-necked people; now therefore let me alone, that my wrath may burn hot against them and I may consume them; but of you I will make a great nation."
>
> But Moses besought the Lord his God, and said, "O Lord, why does thy wrath burn hot against thy people . . . ?" And the Lord repented of the evil which he thought to do to his people. . . .
>
> On the morrow Moses said to the people, "You have sinned a great sin. And now I will go up to the Lord; perhaps I can make atonement for your sin." So Moses returned to the Lord and said, "Alas, this people have sinned a great sin; they have made for themselves gods

of gold. But now, if thou wilt forgive their sin—and if not, blot me, I pray thee, out of thy book which thou hast written." (Ex 32:7-11, 14, 30-32)

The Extent of the Offense

When we consider the full story up to this point, we can see how ungratefully the people behaved. God had delivered them from slavery in Egypt, had drowned their enemies (Pharaoh's army) in the sea while taking them across on dry ground, had provided water, manna, and even quail in the wilderness, and had made a covenant to give them the Promised Land and make them a holy nation. But while Moses was up on the mountain, the people became impatient and behaved as though God did not even exist.

No wonder God was so angry!

Moses, too, was in a rage. As soon as he came down off the mountain and "came near the camp and saw the calf and the dancing, Moses' anger burned hot, and he threw the tables [on which God's Law had been written] out of his hands and broke them at the foot of the mountain. And he took the calf which they had made and burnt it with fire, and ground it to powder, and scattered it upon the water, and made the people of Israel drink it" (Ex 32:19, 20). His rage did not end until three thousand of the most unrepentant offenders were slain (Ex 32:28).

The Extent of the Sacrifice

But, if Moses was so angry, why did he beg God to forgive the people—or if God wasn't willing to forgive, then offer to have God blot *his* name out of the Book of Life instead? Was this some rash, ill-considered declaration? Didn't Moses realize the terrible seriousness of his offer? What was going on?

I think Moses did understand the seriousness of his statement. The Lord meant everything to Moses. After God delivered the people from Pharaoh's army, Moses publicly sang this song: "The Lord is my strength and my song, / and he has become my salvation; / this is my God, and I will praise him, / my father's God, and I will exalt him" (Ex 15:2). Indeed, Moses' entire life had been given over to serving the Lord. For him, there was nothing else of meaning in this life and certainly no hope for a life hereafter apart from the Lord.

Moses knew the gravity of what he was saying. Certainly when Paul said a similar thing, he was fully aware of the eternal consequences: "I could wish that I myself were accursed and cut off from Christ for the sake of my brethren" (Rom 9:3)—if it would have accomplished their salvation. He so loved his Israelite kinsmen that he would have made the supreme sacrifice in order to stand in the gap.

Before he went back up the mountain, Moses told the people, "Perhaps I can make atonement for your sin" (Ex 32:30). The idea of vicarious atonement is found from the very beginning of the Bible. And although, as Psalm 49:7 points out, no mere man can atone for his own sins, let alone the sins of his brother, God was teaching his people to expect a Messiah, a holy Lamb who would qualify as the Redeemer. (Some commentators read Exodus 32:32 to mean, "If you don't forgive the people, then blot me out of the book as well." Even this interpretation shows Moses' willingness to identify with the people, asking God to forgive them or condemn him along with the rest—he was that serious about standing with the people and pleading on their behalf.)

But the most convincing demonstration of the magnitude of Moses' offer was God's response. He did not accept Moses' sacrificial offer ("'Whoever has sinned against me, him will I blot out of my book.'"—verse 33), but God's heart was touched by Moses' plea and his anger softened. He agreed to spare the nation, though he did punish the guilty parties for the sake of their own training, and he substituted his own guiding presence with an angel to go before them on the journey.

How We Stand in the Gap

Moses stood in the gap. A gap is a breech in the defense system, a hole in the wall. God never asked for us to pour cement or bricks or rocks into that hole. The entire call in the Scripture is for a man to stand in the gap.

We Offer to Suffer in Place of Others

We cannot be the atonement for sin as Christ was, but we can play a Christlike sacrificial role. As Paul said, "I rejoice in my sufferings for your sake, and in my flesh I complete what is lacking in Christ's afflictions for the sake of his body, that is, the church" (Col 1:24). That means that my body—and I must take this very literally— becomes part of the defense system. Now the enemy is going to have a go at me. And as long as I stand there, those that I protect—maybe my own children, my church, my nation, maybe the suffering church in Russia, in China, in Iran—will be protected, but I will get the blows.

This is why I think it is so important that we do not ascribe blame to the suffering church around the world, as though their suffering resulted from their own sin. They may be suffering for our sins, not in the sense of the cosmic redemption that Christ accomplished but in the sense that Paul mentioned in Colossians, of completing in their flesh what is necessary for the spread of the gospel, the growth of the church, and reconciliation of sinners.

We Plead with God on Behalf of Others

When Moses appealed to the Lord to forgive the people, you can almost hear the hesitation in his voice: "If thou wilt forgive their sin—and if not...." as if he realized their sin was too great to forgive without proper atonement. Moses realized that God might not forgive the people simply because he asked for it; so he offered the greatest sacrifice he knew, his own relationship with God and his hope of eternal salvation.

Moses himself could not atone for the people; that is why Jesus had to come. In God's plan there had to be a sacrifice so great that on the base of that one sacrifice alone every sin could be forgiven. But it was a personal sacrifice, God's own Son: a person, a body, standing in the gap for us. In Jesus' case it was someone who had never sinned, yet who became sin on behalf of others. And that is why God could accept that sacrifice.

But Moses was Christlike as he offered himself to be an atonement. I'm not suggesting that we should make a similar offer. Calvary has already happened; the price has been paid. But Moses understood what the real spiritual battle was all about, that something had to happen to bridge the gulf between a holy God and sinful man. Someone had to stand in the gap. Someone had to give himself. That is intercession.

Earlier in the chapter Moses demonstrated this form of intercession, of standing in the gap, that is our duty and privilege:

But Moses besought the Lord his God, and said, "O Lord, why does thy wrath burn hot against thy people, whom thou hast brought forth out of the land of Egypt with great power and with a mighty hand? Why should the Egyptians say, 'With evil intent did he bring them forth, to slay them in the mountains, and to consume them from the face of the earth?' Turn from thy fierce wrath, and repent of this evil against thy people. Remember Abraham, Isaac, and Israel, thy servants, to whom thou didst swear by thine own self, and didst say to them, 'I will multiply your descendants as the stars of heaven, and all this land that I have promised I will give to your descendants, and they shall inherit it for ever.'"

(Ex 32:11-13)

Moses seemed to employ three approaches as he pleaded for the people.

He appealed to God's sense of reason by saying, in effect, "You have gone to such great effort to deliver this people, why waste it all now?"

He appealed to God's public relations by pointing out that if God destroyed the Israelites, the heathen would think him cruel since they would never understand God's justification.

He appealed to God's integrity by reminding him of his promises to Abraham, Isaac, and Jacob to bless their descendants.

Prayer is what you do for yourself. I think that's easy. You pray for blessing, protection, health, and all that. But intercession is where your entire effort is for others.

In a similar circumstance, when God was very angry because of the sin of Sodom and Gomorrah, Abraham interceded for the people, pleading with God to save the city if there could be found fifty who were still righteous, then forty-five, then forty, thirty, twenty, and finally ten. And God agreed to save the city if only ten righteous people could be found (Gn 18:27-33).

Standing in the Gap

But what gives any person the right to try to bargain with the Almighty God? I believe you can reason with

God, provided you yourself are willing to pay the price. In Moses' case we see that he was willing to sacrifice his own salvation. His attitude was a willingness to give his own life. He was not speaking in rebellion. He was not threatening: "God, if you wipe out these people, you won't have me either." He was just acting on his tremendous insight into the way God had required a sacrificial lamb—eventually his own Son—to take away the sin of the world.

The Price

God did not require Moses' life or wipe his name from the Book of Life. Moses was not the sinless One, so that would have done no actual good in providing remission for the sins of the people. But apparently God did allow Moses to pay a symbolic price of atonement just as he had instituted the sacrificial lamb in the Old Testament to symbolically foretell the coming of the Lamb of God who would take away the sin of the world.

Moses' greatest desire in his whole life was to walk in the Promised Land. But God did not let him do it. There were apparently two reasons for this. One, Moses struck the rock in anger because of the people's complaints about water, when God had instructed him to speak to the rock (Nm 20:8-12). The second reason, recorded at several points in Scripture, was that God made Moses the *partial* bearer of the people's sin of rebellion (cf. Dt 1:37; 3:23-29; 4:21). There is an acute pathos about this. Moses' one great commission was to take the people to the Promised Land, but he was unable to see its victorious conclusion. It was the burden he bore vicariously for the sin of the people for whom he gave his life, a graphic picture of the suffering servant of Isaiah 53 and Jesus Christ on the cross. It was the suffering of a hero standing in the gap.

The Results

God's response was remarkable, something you seldom hear of or read about. It is found in Exodus 32:14: "So the Lord changed his mind" (TEV). All God is waiting for is for a person to step into the gap and say, "God, let's reason together. What will happen to your great name? How will the enemy talk about you? They will say God failed because his people failed. How about your promises? God, there must be another way."

An intercessor will only reason with God when he or she knows God very personally, knows God's promises, his character, the ways he has dealt with his people in the past. God himself invites us into this intimate relationship: "Come now, let us reason together, says the Lord" (Is 1:18).

The Reward

After this incident of Israel's great idolatry and Moses' intercession, we find recorded the most profound encounter between a man and God to have occurred since the Garden of Eden. Again Moses was up on the mountain with God, and Moses said:

". . . show me now thy ways, that I may know thee and find favor in thy sight. . . ."

And the Lord said to Moses, "This very thing that you have spoken I will do; for you have found favor in my sight, and I know you by name." Moses said, "I pray thee, show me thy glory." And he said, "I will make all my goodness pass before you, and will proclaim before you my name 'The Lord'; . . . But," he said, "you cannot see my face; for man shall not see me and live." And the Lord said, "Behold, there is a place by me where you shall stand upon the rock; and while my glory passes by I will put you in a cleft of the rock, and I will cover you with my hand until I have passed by; then I will take away my hand, and you shall see my back; but my face shall not be seen." (Ex 33:13, 17-23)

What a reward! You see, God loved Moses. The fact that he placed some of his righteous indignation about the people's sin onto Moses' shoulders did not mean that God hated Moses. Moses had found favor in God's sight. God even gave him the privilege of sacrificial suffering.

Shortly before Moses' death the Lord took him to a high mountain on the other side of the Dead Sea on Mount Nebo, which is presently Jordan, and from there he could look over all of the Promised Land. "This is the land of which I swore to Abraham, to Isaac, and to Jacob, 'I will give it to your descendants.' I have let you see it with your eyes, but you shall not go over there" (Dt 34:4).

Centuries later when the fullness of time had come and Jesus, the perfect atonement for sin, was on the scene, this burden was removed from Moses' shoulders. One day Jesus took some of his friends—Peter, James, and John— up on a mountain. There he was transfigured before them—and Moses and Elijah appeared with him. What were they doing there? Luke 9:31 records that they were talking about the work he was going to accomplish on Calvary.

What did Moses know of that? He knew a lot. He had been called to stand in the gap for a time, to receive the blows of sin on behalf of the people. He understood that the day had to come for Christ to be the perfect atonement. And that was why Moses was finally permitted to stand on that mountain with Jesus. He was finally in the Promised Land.

Participating in the Struggle of the Ages

All the attacks of Satan before the transfiguration were his efforts to prevent Jesus from being born in Bethlehem or from reaching the cross. All the attacks of Satan after Jesus rose from the dead have been against the church to thwart the purpose of God in spreading the gospel to every people. Satan hopes thereby to prevent Christ from returning in victory.

We are not here for our own benefit. We are here to take an active part in this great struggle of the ages. Our task is to proclaim the Kingdom of God, to establish its principles and rescue people from the devil's grasp by telling them of God's saving power. To that end we are to become intercessors, and in so doing we may have to stand in the gap on behalf of people who otherwise would perish, people who need protection, people whose protection has been taken away because of persecution, people who have grown weak because of personal sin.

Intercession is just the opposite of fatalism. Too many Christians today are fatalistic: "What will be, will be." They even claim their passivity is a surrender to the will of God. Nonsense! A thousand times a day we act to have our own will done. But when we think we cannot have any influence on decisions we say, "Well, the will of the Lord be done." We need to become fighters for God, to stand up for righteousness against injustice and immorality. We must have a relationship with God in which we talk things over with him; we must have insight into God's ways and his desires.

While in Prague, Czechoslovakia, in 1955, I visited a small Moravian church with about forty young people in attendance. Things were very restrictive at that time. Many believers had been forced out of their jobs or denied education because of their faith. They were looked on as unpatriotic.

After encouraging these believers, I was given a small gift and told to take it back to my home in Holland. It was a small, silver lapel ornament in the shape of a cup.

"This," I was told, "is the symbol of the church in Czechoslovakia. We call it the cup of suffering. Now you are a partaker of that cup. When people ask you about it, tell them about us and remind them that we are part of the Body of Christ, too, and that we are in pain."

As I have worn this pin, many around the world have remembered to intercede for these and other believers behind the Iron Curtain. Maybe we have been privileged to stand in the gap on their behalf. Does such intercession have any benefit in our modern world? I believe it does. Though conditions are still very restrictive and pre-carious, there has been much change for the better.

In 1987, for instance, a number of religious prisoners were unexpectedly released in the Soviet Union, cutting almost in half the numbers of believers known to be in prison for religious activity. The Soviet government promised to permit the printing of 100,000 Bibles inside the Soviet Union and the shipment of an additional 100,000 Bibles from the outside. Konstantin Kharchev, the chairman of the Soviet Council for Religious Affairs, has stated that excessively restrictive laws need to change. Possibly for the first time he has admitted officially that the government was responsible for closing thousands of churches. (For more information, read Chris Woehr, "Soviet Official Claims Conditions for Christians to Improve, Prisoners Will Be Freed," in *Open Doors News Service,* Sept. 10, 1987, pp. 2, 3.) The prayers of believers around the world are being answered.

We praise God when his light breaks into the shadows of sin and suffering. But Satan is determined to keep people in darkness, and 66 percent of the world's population continues to live under conditions that restrict their free exercise of worship and belief as we know it. Heroes of the faith are still needed to stand in the gap. Will you be one?

THREE

Gideon: A Hero's Quest for Truth

A COUNTRY MUCH IN THE NEWS in recent years is Afghanistan. Recently, a conference on missions was held in the Middle East. Focusing on Afghanistan, a nation where, like some other countries in the Arab block, there has never been a national church as far as we know, the question was asked, "Why has there never been a church in Afghanistan?" There was great silence. After a long while an old gray-haired missionary stood up and with a faltering voice said, "Maybe it is because no one has ever laid down his life for Afghanistan."

I think he touched on the secret. Heroes of faith are those that go aggressively into areas where there is no church or where there is a suffering church or where the gospel has never been preached, but they go with a willingness to lay down their lives. And sometimes effectiveness comes only when they actually do lay down their lives.

Many countries in our world today are in great spiritual and physical need. More than half of the world is closed off from traditional missionary work because of political and religious restrictions. When we realize there are billions who have never heard of Christ, we say, "God, it is still your world." There *will* come a time when the kingdoms of this world will become the Kingdom of Jesus Christ, and to that end we must work.

As I read the Scriptures I recognize the world in which we live, the problems we face, and people with whom I can identify. I see how timid and cowardly they were, but still God put his hand on them and said, "I want to use you." When I see those parallels, God speaks to me and says, "You can do the same. You can have a lasting impact on the situations in your world."

Times Like Ours

The story of Gideon, which begins in Judges 6, provides such a parallel. The children of Israel were now in the land of Canaan, and God had told them clearly to drive out the inhabitants and claim the land. Some of the tribes drove out the Canaanites from their allotted territory, but others failed to finish the job. God warned them that these people and their gods would be "thorns in your side" and "a snare to you" (Jgs 2:3). Then Joshua, and the generation that had entered the land with him so victoriously, died, and the generation that came after them forsook the Lord God and began to worship Baal and other Canaanite gods.

Israel continued to fight their enemies, but because of their disobedience God withdrew his hand of protection, and they were continually harassed, plundered, and beaten. Nonetheless, God raised up judges among them—righteous men and women who listened to God, spoke his word to the people, and helped deliver them from their enemies. Sometimes the people listened to the judges and experienced victory and peace; but usually they returned to their evil ways and were once again in trouble.

These are circumstances we have no trouble recognizing. In the days of the judges, as in our own time, everyone did what was right in their own eyes (see Jgs 17:6 and 21:25). It, too, was an age in which the people did not recognize a fixed point of moral reference outside of themselves; they did not acknowledge the Law of God as their standard; they made their own rules. Does this sound disturbingly familiar to what we see and hear all around us today?

Just before we meet young Gideon, God had allowed the people to prosper and have peace for forty years, but then "The people of Israel [again] did what was evil in the sight of the Lord; and the Lord gave them into the hand of Midian seven years. . . . Israel was brought very low because of Midian; and the people of Israel cried for help to the Lord" (Jgs 6:1, 6). When we study the chapter, we find that the people could only function under the cover of darkness. They threshed their wheat at night; their supplies were locked up and hidden; everything had to be done in secret.

In more than half the world this is exactly the situation that people live in today!

In the midst of their distress, Israel had sense enough to call upon God. That's the wonderful thing about the grace of God. He never reproaches anyone who cries to him after messing up his or her own life. Once you understand God's character, you know you can count on him. You never have to feel bad about turning to him, no matter what sin you've committed, because he is always ready to forgive the truly repentant soul. Nor does he call back a record of your past sins that have been forgiven and covered by the blood of Jesus. You can always come back to the Father.

The people of Israel cried to the Lord, and God answered by giving them a godly leader. When God answers our plea for forgiveness, he doesn't just forgive and forget us. He answers by giving us instructions, telling us how to go on in righteousness, building up our character, making us men and women of God who can not only conquer sin in our private lives but by example become leaders of others. And why not? The great need today is for Christian leaders.

But, as we will see in the story of Gideon, godly leadership is not necessarily based on our own qualifications. It is based on God's plan for his people, on our understanding of his ways with man, and on our willingness to be obedient.

The Truth That Sets Us Free

When the people cried to the Lord, he first of all sent a prophet to tell them what really had been going on. When we are in trouble, our perspective is often limited just like the Israelites: we see the enemy attacking or oppressing us, and we call for help. But that's not always the whole picture. This is what the prophet told the people:

> "Thus says the Lord, the God of Israel: I led you up from Egypt, and brought you out of the house of bondage; and I delivered you from the hand of the Egyptians, and from the hand of all who oppressed you, and drove them out before you, and gave you their land; and I said to you, 'I am the Lord your God; you shall not pay reverence to the gods of the Amorites, in whose land you dwell.' But you have not given heed to my voice." (Jgs 6:8-10)

The prophet laid out the truth: God had set the people up in a peaceful and secure situation and instructed them not to worship the pagan gods. Now they were being overrun by the Midianites. Were they being oppressed because God had let down on his end of the bargain? No; the truth was that they had disobeyed him.

Often we are in the same situation. We think we are

being persecuted unjustly, but too often we are reaping what we have sown. Satan certainly is our enemy, always on the prowl to knock us down. But we tend to forget that we cannot sow weeds and then pray for a good harvest. When we sow rubbish we're going to harvest rubbish. If we want a good harvest, we must sow good seed. When we have sown the seeds of sin, the first thing we need is the truth. Until we accept the truth about our own attitudes and actions, there is no possibility for true freedom. But the truth is often hard to accept.

The Encounter with Truth

The second thing God did in answer to the cries of the people was send "the angel of the Lord" to enlist a young man named Gideon in the task of leading Israel to freedom.

While any angel sent to execute the commands of God might be called an angel of the Lord, the references in the Old Testament to "*the* angel of the Lord" occur under circumstances which seem to signify that the same exceptional emissary is meant in every instance. Some scholars even feel that the preincarnate Christ is meant. But in any case, this heavenly messenger spoke with the full authority of the Lord himself.

God's Different View of Us

Imagine the scene. It was Gideon's job to thresh the wheat, but because of the danger he was doing it in his father's wine press. A stranger came and sat under an oak tree nearby, maybe watched him working for awhile. Then the stranger—God's messenger—said something that Gideon thought was very strange: "The Lord is with you, you mighty man of valor" (Jgs 6:12).

Now Gideon was threshing his wheat in secret for fear

of the enemy; he was a scared young man. But the angel of the Lord said that God was with him and called him a valiant warrior. This shows that God looks at us in a totally different way than we look at ourselves. And only what God sees in us is important.

It doesn't matter if I'm a stuttering Dutchman who has trouble with the English language. It doesn't matter that you can find scores of other weaknesses in me or in yourself. God has a different way of looking at you and me. God sees the potential. In fact, God saw our potential before you became a Christian, even before you were born. And God builds all the circumstances of your life based on what he sees as the potential in your life. That's why God's ways with men and women are so surprising and so totally different from what we might do. We may not see anything at all in our children or in our pastor or the person sitting next to us in church. But God, who sees the end from the beginning, steps in and calls us based on the potential he sees. It's a revelation, a word from Heaven that, under the circumstances, no man would ever invent: "The Lord is with you, you mighty man of valor."

Understanding the Lord

How confused Gideon's initial reaction must have been. I mean, suppose God said that to you today. Maybe just yesterday you didn't have the courage to witness to somebody even though you had a good chance, and today God says, "You're a mighty warrior."

"Did I hear that right, Lord? Did you say that?"

What would your reaction be—to argue with God or to agree with him?

It's important for us to know that God didn't make us to be robots. God chose to make us rational people partially so that we would make the effort to understand him and his ways—a response far above that of a robot. God even wants to go further, as he did with Abraham when he called him "my friend" (Is 41:8). God wants to talk to you as with a friend, and you must talk to him as with a friend, also. But don't say you understand the Lord if you don't. It's true that sometimes we need to obey even when we don't understand. But don't be afraid to ask questions. Gideon wasn't. He didn't understand the angel's greeting, and he had a few questions he wanted to ask God:

> "Pray, sir, if the Lord is with us, why then has all this befallen us? And where are all his wonderful deeds which our fathers recounted to us, saying, 'Did not the Lord bring us up from Egypt?' But now the Lord has cast us off, and given us into the hand of Midian." (Jgs 6:13)

That was a very good question. Gideon was respectful, but he did not piously accept that God was with them. He wanted to understand the truth. He wanted to understand why it did not *appear* that God was with them.

No Promise Box Hero

Some people take Matthew 28:20, where Jesus said, "I am with you always," and they frame it, put it on their mantel, and say, "Isn't it wonderful that Jesus is always with us?" But look at the context of *how* he is with us; "... in *power and authority*" (v. 18). That is, while Jesus is always "with us" and able to hear our cry of repentance or need, his blessing, his power and authority, are not necessarily with us when we are in a place where we shouldn't be. The context of the promise in Matthew begins with Jesus commanding us to "Go . . . and make disciples of all nations." It is in *that* context that he promised to be with us always.

If things aren't the way they should be, ask God why. Discover the truth. Gideon's reaction was the correct one. Many of us have heard a lot of pious talk in our lives. We've been to many church services, heard many choirs sing. Maybe your mother bought you a nice little promise box with all those nice Bible verses in it—the ones that only speak of blessings, of course. They never tell us to repent; they never tell what must be done to get the blessing. They are the lazy man's Bible.

But we can't live on promise boxes. We need to discover the truth. If Gideon hadn't raised the issue of what had gone wrong, nothing would have changed in Israel. Nothing would have changed in his own life. But he said, "God, if what you say is true, then tell me where all the miracles are that my fathers told me about. I cannot live on the miracles that you did for my fathers; I need miracles in my own life. I cannot just study the revivals of the past; I need revival today. I can't live on the blessings you gave my father; I need blessings for my family. Where are those miracles if the Lord is with us?"

Gideon's Own Strength

Do we dare to ask God questions about the things that trouble our life? "If you are with us today, Lord, then where are all the miracles? Why can't I send my daughter across the street at night? Why can't I leave my car unlocked? Why do I see so many homeless in my city? Why are teenagers committing suicide? Why are we so afraid?"

Where are the miracles? Where is the blessing? Where are the revivals? Where is the protection of Almighty God? I wish that we *would* ask those questions, friends. Let's be frank with God; let's be honest about how we feel. *But only if we're prepared to hear the truth, and act on it.*

The Right Question Yields the Right Answer

Unless we start asking the right questions, nothing will change. Gideon obviously asked the right question because God replied: "Go in this might of yours and deliver Israel from the hand of Midian; do not I send you?" (Jgs 6:14).

God certainly did send Gideon; he even made a point to prove this to Israel in the very first battle against the Midianites. The Lord told Gideon to cut the size of his army time and again until he had a ridiculously small band of only three hundred men to go up against an enemy whose camp "lay along the valley like locusts for multitude" (Jgs 7:12). When Gideon's band defeated the Midianites, there was no question that the victory was a miracle from God.

But in this first encounter with the heavenly messenger, God also told Gideon to "Go in this might of yours." What might was that? What strength did Gideon possess? He reminded God that he wasn't anything much: "Behold, my clan is the weakest in Manasseh, and I am the least in my family" (Jgs 6:15). I believe Gideon's might was his willingness to seek out the truth and act on it. He was a man God could trust not to claim false glory for himself. He had not piously accepted anything he wasn't sure belonged to him, not even the title of "a mighty man of valor." God seemed to be saying, "I love it. I love a truth-seeker. I need a man who knows that his strength must come from God. This is the attitude I look for. Go in *that* strength. That is the mighty quality you possess."

Applying the Truth at Home

Once convinced that Israel's troubles were self-imposed by their disobedience and idol worship, and that God was calling him to do something about it, Gideon began by applying the truth at home. Centuries later,

Jesus told us to start spreading the gospel at home—in our own "Jerusalem." It's the best place to start. If we can't declare the truth at home, we'll have little success in a foreign setting.

So at the Lord's command, Gideon took ten of his men to tear down the altar to the false god, Baal—right there in his father's front yard!

Now it's true that Gideon was fearful. He did it at night because "he was too afraid of his family and the men of the town to do it by day" (Jgs 6:27). But remember, God knows us better than we know ourselves. God never said Gideon lacked fear. Dedication to truth was Gideon's strong point, and based on that, God trusted him to get the job done, in spite of his fear. And he did it. He got moving.

Don't think that with the first step you land at your destination. In personal victories you must go step by step. That night Gideon was still a bit afraid. But he pulled the thing down; he attacked the enemy. There was action, and God blessed it.

Maybe we ought to define the term "courage." Courage (or valor) is not the absence of fear; it is pressing on in spite of fear. Men and women of God—heroes of faith—are not people who are necessarily fearless; they are just people who do what needs to be done.

Others Are Freed by Truth

Prior to Gideon's action the whole countryside was in bondage to the falsehood brought on by their sin. They were oppressed by the Midianites and their minds were captured by the false god, Baal. But Gideon's actions on behalf of truth began to free the people; the first was his father. Many in the town were angry and wanted to avenge Baal. But Gideon's father, Joash, defended his son: "If [Baal] is a god, let him contend for himself, because his altar has been pulled down" (Jgs 6:31). Joash was freed by the truth. It was not long before others were likewise freed by the truth and were willing to rally to Gideon's call when he prepared to fight the Midianites.

Joash's defense challenges me as a father, and should challenge all of us parents. Are we really behind our children? Are we brave enough to let our children go into the world and face danger for the sake of the truth? Let's stand behind them and say, "Children, I am with you. You want to go to the mission field? You are called to do a dangerous job for God? Good. Go and serve God. Give your life for Afghanistan or Iran or Cuba or China. Your father and mother are behind you. We don't want to try to keep you home just because it is going to be dangerous."

Then Comes God's Spirit

After taking the first step of action, something very wonderful happened to Gideon. The enemy began to move, to come together, to threaten God's people. "But the spirit of the Lord took possession of Gideon; and he sounded the trumpet" (Jgs 6:34). And then the people of God began to move, to come together, to commit themselves to action.

This is the real secret. It's the spirit-filled life, the spirit-anointed ministry, that's finally going to make the change.

Gideon opened the way by pursuing the truth, and then the Spirit of the Lord took possession of him. Scripture doesn't say anything about him first doing a study on the Holy Spirit, as good as that might be. Instead, it was his sheer obedience to the truth that resulted in his baptism in the Holy Spirit.

Gideon continued testing for the truth. He did what God told him to do, but he also asked God to confirm the truth of his instructions by what we now call "putting out a fleece." Gideon actually put out a sheepskin (fleece) and asked God to make it wet with dew when the ground around was dry; then he asked for the ground to be wet and the fleece dry (see Judges 6:36-40). You would think God would get impatient with him as though Gideon's requests were expressions of constant doubt. But God knew Gideon. His quest was an honest search for truth, proven by his subsequent obedience.

Too often we piously ask no questions of God, but we don't do anything either. Or we ask questions, we "put out a fleece," because we're looking for a way out. We don't want to take action; we don't really want to obey.

But today God needs heroes of the faith like Gideon, who are willing to discover why the people of God are being oppressed by the enemy on every front. God needs men and women who are willing to ask the right questions, and then act on God's truth. And if we do this, God will give us the confidence we need to step out and take action.

Gideon's victories were not won with the power of a mighty army, nor will we win any victories this way. Rather, God delivers his people with a small band of dedicated people led by men and women in search of truth and willing to act in the power that comes with obedience.

FOUR

David: Conquering with the Right Weapon

WHEN YOU THINK ABOUT HEROES of the faith, what comes to mind? Great spiritual battles with demons? Fire called down from heaven? But some of the greatest spiritual battles are fought only with words. This makes the Word of God a very precious thing.

Once when I was in the Soviet Union I met a Russian Christian named Joseph. He told me that he had been in a labor camp for ten years. As we talked, I discovered that while in prison camp he had made a most unique Bible. It was his job to empty cement bags; he would tear off pieces of the thick brown paper from the cement bags and, with a pencil he'd found, write on them every Bible verse he could recall.

"I managed to fill twelve pages with these verses," he said. "Often when I was alone in a quiet corner, I would be joined by other Christians. Then I would open my shirt, pull out my cement-bag Bible, and we would read the verses together."

How he loved that Bible! My eyes filled with tears as he placed it in my hands for me to examine.

A saying attributed to Karl Marx is, "Give me twenty-six lead soldiers, and I will conquer the world." He was referring, of course, to the twenty-six letters of the alphabet to be found in a printer's type bin. But those same twenty-six letters also can form the Words of Life. Seeing how valuable Joseph's cement-bag Bible was to him and how it had sustained his faith and the faith of others in a time of great trial caused me to commit myself even more deeply to helping all people have access to God's Word.

A Battle of Words

One of the greatest battles in the Bible involved a weapon we all know: words. It's the story of David and Goliath told in 1 Samuel 17.

> Now the Philistines gathered their armies for battle; and they were gathered at Socoh, which belongs to Judah, and encamped between Socoh and Azekah, in Ephesdammim. And Saul and the men of Israel were gathered, and encamped in the valley of Elah, and drew up in line of battle against the Philistines. And the Philistines stood on the mountain on the one side, and Israel stood on the mountain on the other side, with a valley between them. (1 Sm 17:1-3)

Imagine the situation. On one side of the valley were the Philistines, armed to the teeth. On the other stood the army of Israel—with just sticks and clubs for weapons! Why weren't they prepared? Because the Philistines who occupied Israel had driven the blacksmiths from the land so there would be no chance for them to forge swords or spears. When an Israelite needed to sharpen his ax or sickle, he had to go meekly down to the Philistine's camp and pay for the sharpening. Only the king and his son had any personal armor (see 1 Samuel 13:19-22).

Think about the humiliation that the enemy inflicted

on God's people by telling them they couldn't have weapons or train their young men for battle. Compare that to the spiritual situation today. How outrageous for any atheistic government to determine how many Bibles the church can have in a particular country. How scandalous that any secular authority should restrict God's people from training their children in the ways of the Lord. Is the enemy going to tell us, God's people, how we are going to behave? Is the enemy going to curtail our activity so that we cannot obey God's Word to win the world? Recognize the situation?

Almost the only thing the Israelites could do was talk.

The Power of Words

But that's exactly what the Philistines were doing, too. Their champion Goliath strutted out onto the battlefield, "six cubits and a span" (1 Sm 17:4). If the biblical cubit equaled eighteen inches, as most scholars think, then Goliath stood a threatening nine and a half feet tall. Yet all he hurled were words: taunts, insults, accusations.

> He stood and shouted to the ranks of Israel, "Why have you come out to draw up for battle? Am I not a Philistine, and are you not servants of Saul? Choose a man for yourselves, and let him come down to me. If he is able to fight with me and kill me, then we will be your servants; but if I prevail against him and kill him, then you shall be our servants and serve us. . . . I defy the ranks of Israel this day." (1 Sm 17: 8-10)

Every morning, every night, Goliath shouted the same insults. He was actually insulting God, for it was well understood among ancient peoples that their strength or weakness in battle was an expression of the strength of their god. Therefore, this defiance was hurled at the God of Israel just as much as at the men in the army. We must not underestimate the impact of this kind of propaganda. For forty days, every morning and every evening, he shouted at the Israelites so that all could hear. There was no escaping it. Eighty times he delivered the same evil message: "You can never win! You'll never be helped! You'll never be free from sin; you'll always be lost. You'll never make it; you'll always be slaves!" I call it brainwashing, and it had a powerful effect. The Israelites were so paralyzed by fear that they didn't even dare to name the enemy. Instead, they said, "Have you seen this man who has come up?" (1 Sm 17:25).

Seeing through a Challenge

This situation didn't change until a young man named David arrived on the scene. His father had sent him to the Israelite camp to visit his brothers and bring word about their welfare. When David arrived, the Israelite army was making a show of going to the battle line, but turned and fled when Goliath issued his taunting challenge. In tune with God's will, David immediately knew that the situation was not right in God's eyes.

This is the first step heroes of the faith must take: seeking God's will with the intent of acting on it. If we study the Bible merely for our own salvation or just to show off our great knowledge of the Word, it won't do us or anyone else any good. We must be in contact with God with the goal of changing the situation around us. Then we will see life as God sees it.

Once David arrived, the real battle began. Shocked by the fear of those supposedly on God's side, he immediately expressd his indignation: "For who is this uncircumcised Philistine, that he should defy the armies of the living God?" (1 Sm 17:26).

David immediately called his bluff. This giant had no part in the Kingdom of God. How did David know? By the blasphemous words Goliath spoke. David was not afraid to identify him for what he was. He made a theological issue of it because it was a spiritual battle. It had nothing to do with the Philistines and Israel simply as civil nations. There was something far more important at stake: the honor of God. A holy indignation took hold of David; he could not restrain himself any more. He got mad. There was something burning within him, and he had to act.

Only that which burns inside you will come out in action.

Keeping the Issues Straight

The good news spread quickly through the camp: someone was accepting Goliath's challenge! Before long, King Saul heard that a hero of the faith had arrived. Was there hope for Israel after all? Saul sent for him. When he arrived, David declared, "Let no man's heart fail because of him; your servant will go and fight with this Philistine" (1 Sm 17:32).

As has happened so often with the church, David found that Israel had gone into battle unprepared, without proper weapons. Only Saul and his son Jonathan had any weapons at all. But David focused on the real solution: to fight in the power of the Lord. That was the type of fighting he knew. But Saul had been so brainwashed that he didn't see things that way. All he could see was that David was a youth—no match for the seasoned warrior giant.

David tried to give the king a vision of what it was like to fight in the power of the Lord by reviewing his past experience:

"Your servant used to keep sheep for his father; and when there came a lion, or a bear, and took a lamb from the flock, I went after him and smote him and delivered it out of his mouth; and if he arose against me, I caught him by his beard, and smote him and killed him. Your servant has killed both lions and bears; and this uncircumcised Philistine shall be like one of them, seeing he has defied the armies of the living God." (1 Sm 17:34-37)

Again, David kept the issues straight. This was a spiritual conflict. It was the enemy's defiance of God that elicited David's action—not personal gain, not saving face, not even the physical freedom of the Hebrew people. The key to his success was that he acted on spiritual principle.

We Can't Always Prevent the Evil of Others

David's review of his past history revealed another important insight. Notice that even though David was present when the lamb was taken, he couldn't prevent it from happening. He could only take action afterward.

We all have to live in a world of realities. There really is an Iron Curtain, persecution, terrorism, famine, poverty. We haven't been able to prevent those kinds of things. Nor was David able to keep the lion and bear from coming into the flock.

What made him especially indignant, however, was that the sheep were not his, but his father's. That's the sense of responsibility that must be ours as well. Where are the Christians who are willing to take care of the sheep just because they belong to our heavenly Father?

Carrying Out Our Duty

We consider David to be courageous, but all he did was carry out his duty, no matter what it cost him. He was responsible for the safety and health of these sheep, and the lion and bear had no business coming into his father's flock.

It's tempting to think, "What's more important: the life of one lamb or David's life?" That's typical Western thinking, but it's not how God thinks. Our life is worth nothing if we neglect our duty and fail in our responsibilities. We will never see miracles or God's intervention if we are more worried about ourselves than our calling. David's perspective was: "I did it because those sheep belonged to my father."

Often we calculate risks and then decide not to get involved, leaving the weak, the vulnerable, the threatened, to defend themselves. But they cannot. That's why such a large portion of the world is suffering: under injustice, violence, persecution, and racism. Here David sets an example for us to follow.

At first King Saul was disappointed to find that David was only a youth—hardly a match, he thought, for the terrifying warrior giant. But David's testimony impressed Saul. He realized he had finally found one man who would act on principle, armed with God's presence and power. That's all it takes to be a hero of the faith. With God, we can do all things.

Inner Integrity Produces Outward Strength

Because of his personal experience, David had confidence in the Lord's power to deliver him, and because of his inner strength, he gave faith to the king that he could succeed where everyone else had failed. His private life of discipline, devotion, and faithfulness meant that he could succeed in the public arena.

The faith that David inspired in Saul was considerable. If David failed as Israel's champion, the terms that Goliath had announced were that Israel would become the Philistines' servants. It is not obvious whether that would have been any worse than the situation that already existed, but it was a serious thing to let this shepherd youth represent all Israel. Think how desperate they must have been!

Trying to be helpful, Saul gave David his own armor, which he should have been using to fight Goliath himself. We know from Scripture that Saul was a very big man— head and shoulders above most others. The fact that he even attempted to put his helmet and coat of mail on David suggests that David wasn't particularly small. But the Bible says that "he was not used to them" and took the armor off.

In fact, Saul's weapons were worse than useless to David; they would have encumbered him and put him at a distinct disadvantage. He didn't need Saul's outward armament. God had called David as a shepherd boy, not a heavily-armed warrior. When God calls us, it's to come just as we are. Don't try to do great things in someone else's capacity. We can only be effective in God's service if we yield ourselves as we are, not pretending to be anything else.

Confronting the Giant

Finally it was time for David to tackle the giant. Goliath made his eightieth appearance to taunt the Israelites and their God, but this time something was different. There was a shepherd boy in front of him, with a sling and five smooth stones.

Did you ever wonder why he picked five stones? Was he afraid he would miss the first few times and might need some more ammunition? I don't think so. I think he chose five stones because Goliath had four brothers, including the giant who had six fingers on each hand and six toes on each foot (2 Sm 21:20-22; 1 Chr 20:4-8). David was implying that he was not only going to challenge one enemy but he was ready to deal with all the enemies of Israel.

Heroes of the faith are men and women of God who believe in total victory. There should be no negotiated compromises with evil. With five smooth stones, David demonstrated to all of Israel that if the nation turned in faith to God, they could be delivered from all their enemies.

As David walked up to Goliath, the Philistine boomed, "Am I a dog, that you come at me with sticks?" Actually, the answer was "yes!" David's advance was a statement that there was no place in the kingdom for a man like Goliath, the enemy of God himself.

Spiritual Battles Require Spiritual Weapons

Goliath looked upon David with undisguised contempt, but David responded with the very weapon Goliath had used to intimidate Israel: words. Although Goliath was heavily armed with a huge spear and javelin and an armor bearer just to hold up his shield, he never had the chance to use them.

Spiritual battles are never fought with material weapons but with principles. They are battles for people's minds and souls, and most often they are fought with words. David didn't mince his.

"You come to me with a sword and with a spear and with a javelin; but I come to you in the name of the Lord of hosts, the God of the armies of Israel, whom you have defied. This day the Lord will deliver you into my hand, and I will strike you down, and cut off your head; I will give the dead bodies of the host of the Philistines this day to the birds of the air and to the wild beasts of the earth; that all the earth may know that there is a God in Israel, and that all this assembly may know that the Lord saves not with sword and spear; for the battle is the Lord's and he will give you into our hand." (1 Sm 17:45-47)

Wouldn't that have been something to hear? This shepherd boy stood before an awesome fighting machine with only one special weapon: the Word of God. The battle was the Lord's, but David still had to fight it. He fought not with just any words but with *God's* Word. The moment he proclaimed the Word of God, it became God's responsibility to give him the victory.

The outcome of the fight was exactly as David said it would be. Goliath was killed, the Philistines were routed, and Israel was freed. But did you ever wonder why the whole Philistine army fled when only one man had gone down? From a human perspective it could have been a lucky shot from a lone boy with a few rocks. Certainly the Philistines' physical dominance over unarmed Israel was not dependent on one man, no matter how big he was. But the reason they fled was because the real battle was never a physical one anyway. It was a spiritual fight— between the God of Israel and the forces of evil. Therefore, God's victory was made all the more dramatic by the contrast between a boy with some rocks and the highly skilled warrior giant. Ancient people understood the spiritual implications of this conflict as many modern people cannot; that is why the Philistines fled in terror.

If only we Christians had that same spiritual insight! But too often we get confused and think that our security is based on the tanks and bombs, courts and economics of the countries in which we live. But it's the proclamation of the Word of God that makes the difference in the world. Without the courage of one young man to stand up "in the name of the Lord of hosts," Israel would have been in chains.

Something More Precious Than Life

I think of another hero, Patrick Henry, who stood in St. John's Church in Richmond, Virginia, in 1775 and stated his principles, despite the cost:

Gentlemen may cry peace, peace, but there is no peace. War is actually begun; our brethren are already in the field. How can we stand idle? Is life so dear, or peace so sweet, as to be purchased at the price of chains and slavery? Forbid it, Almighty God. I know not what course others may take, but as for me, give me liberty or give me death.

It's time that Christians all over the world commit themselves to a war of independence, a spiritual war in which our own lives and happiness don't count so much. I wrote a book about this, taking a line from Patrick Henry, and titled it, *Is Life So Dear?*

David didn't count his life to be so dear that he couldn't stand up for the name of the Lord God. He didn't think and plan and scheme. As when he went after the lamb in the lion's jaws, he knew his heavenly Father would feel ashamed of him if he ran away from danger rather than doing his duty.

Our calling is to use our wealth and knowledge and resources to spread the Word of God to nations that are enslaved, where the lion and bear have already come in. We have to admit that we were unable to prevent the situation; the world is full of realities we can't get away from. It was a reality that the Philistines were in the land of Judah, only ten miles west of Jerusalem. But there was also the tremendous reality that God had a young hero prepared to give his all.

The situation today has been given to us, but it's our

duty to change it. God wants us to become warriors. Is that what we're doing?

The Cost of Victory

Unfortunately, I believe that too many of us are playing spiritual Monopoly instead. We throw the dice and move along the board: "Go directly to Pentecost; do not stop at Gethsemane; do not stop at Calvary; pick up your hundred dollars." It's a deadly game, both for our effectiveness in the Kingdom and for the salvation of the world.

When I travel in communist countries I often meet young pastors who want to leave their country for the "free" West, preferably the United States. But I always say, "Don't do it. If God has given you the responsibility to be a pastor, stay with your sheep; you should not flee. You must stay where you are and serve God. You can fight for God best where his enemies are strongest. If you flee from the battlefield and try to avoid the conflict, then you will not only be less effective, but you may also leave the place of his divine protection for you."

The Danger of Pursuing Self-Interest

You see, I have discovered that many who leave their countries for a "safer" place often lose their faith. God has equipped them for the kind of fight they are in, but they are often not prepared to contend with the spiritual warfare of the materialistic society into which they go.

I once shared this advice with a congregation in Cuba. A pastor came up after my sermon, and in front of the hushed audience he said, "Brother Andrew, I have been planning to leave Cuba for America. My application papers are already being processed, but after what I heard you say about a shepherd staying with the flock, I have decided before God tonight to stay."

The congregation rose up as one and clapped their hands. They said, "Gracias, Padre; O gracias, Padre." They were so happy that this man was going to stay. I later heard that he was greatly used by the Lord in Cuba.

There Will Be Pain

To be heroes of the faith, we must come into the battle realizing that indeed there will be suffering and wounds, pain and death. That's only being realistic. How can warfare be otherwise?

This marvelous story of David tells how one man changed the course of Israel's history and—as an ancestor of Jesus—our spiritual destiny as well. Admittedly, he wasn't an ordinary man, but nobody else knew that at the time. Saul, David's brothers, and Goliath all considered him to be of no account. When we're looking around for heroes, our tendency is to look for someone well known, above average, highly educated—certainly God *has* to do something great through that person. Nonsense! The heroes of the faith are often ordinary people, like you and me.

I'll never forget the 1966 World Conference on Evangelism that I attended in Berlin. The list of speakers was most impressive. Some people required an entire page to document their accomplishments, how famous they were, how many books they had written. Yet as I paged through the scores of professors and doctors, I spotted one familiar name: Corrie ten Boom, Watchmaker.

Now, more than twenty years later, I've forgotten all the others, but I still remember Corrie. All that week, in that huge congress hall, wherever you saw a crowd of people, there was Corrie in the middle, ministering. She was not a professor, had no degrees, but she was a heroine of the faith. She knew God's principles, had acted on them, and paid the price.

David, too, paid a price. His wasn't an easy victory, and his pitiful little stones were certainly not weapons to impress the world. But he came in the name of the Lord, and because of that, the victory was his.

Are we willing to be heroes of the faith and proclaim the Word of the Lord, no matter what it costs us? If God could give a victory through David, he can do it through us. David had only a small part of the Old Testament to draw on, but he proclaimed it boldly. With the complete Old and New Testaments, multiplied translations, commentaries, great preachers, television, and radio, why haven't we conquered the world for Christ?

Let's decide together that we will be heroes of the faith. God gives faith freely to anyone who wants to receive it and walk in his way. Are we willing to go out into a very dangerous world with only one weapon, the Sword of the Spirit? You may not be able to see it or feel its sharp edge, but it will make you invincible. No Iron Curtain, cultural curtain, or religious curtain can keep out those who move with the Word of God.

Enemies come with their pitiful weapons, but we come in the name of the Lord. The victory is ours!

FIVE

Jonah: The Reluctant Hero

WHEN I FIRST WENT TO THE SOVIET UNION over thirty years ago, there were still thousands of pastors without a Bible. I preached in a great many churches where no one in the congregation could look up the text of my sermon. The believers in those churches prayed fervently that somehow God would send them a Bible.

On one of my journeys in Russia I was told of a church where they had been praying for many years for a copy of the Word of God—just one copy. One day God answered their prayer: a courier came to that town and delivered a Bible to the pastor.

We will probably never understand the joy and excitement those people felt because for the first time their pastor had his own copy of the Word of God. How he must have loved it! How he must have cried and wept, and hugged and kissed that precious Bible. I know that's how these people respond because I've seen them do it.

Then Sunday came, and in that crowded church the pastor got up and showed his Bible. There were great shouts of "hallelujah" all over the congregation. What joy, what gratefulness, what praise to God Almighty! I'm sure that the sermon he preached that morning was greatly improved because he had the text in hand.

At the end of the service, however, he did something I could never have done. He stepped down to the congregation and began to tear the pages out of his Bible, giving them to the people. Everyone in that congregation got a page from the only Bible he had ever owned. Everyone in the church went home that day with the printed Word, a part of the Scriptures.

Later that week the pastor was walking in town, and he met a man from the congregation who greeted him with a broad smile, bigger than ever. "My brother," he said, "you must have received a good page last Sunday."

The man's eyes shone as he said, "Oh, Pastor, what a page I got; you won't believe it."

"Well, what did you get?"

"I got a page from Jeremiah."

"Oh," the pastor said. "That's too bad. Jeremiah was a prophet of doom, you know, persecuted because he announced the judgment of God on an unrighteous people. He was arrested, beaten, tortured. He was thrown in a pit, and eventually killed while in exile. Not a very encouraging book, is it?"

"On the contrary, Pastor; it's very encouraging to me. You know what it says? Jeremiah said, 'And the word of the Lord came to me.' Pastor, if it can come to Jeremiah, it can come to me, too. This is God's message for me."

"But surely . . . Listen, wouldn't you like something different. Here, I have a page from Matthew. Take it. I'll trade it with you for the rest of the week."

"Oh, please, no," said the man. "The fact that the Word of God comes to me, that has changed my life."

That's how we should respond. The fact that the Word of God comes to us in this mixed up, confused, sinful, lawless world of ours can make such a difference in our lives. Will we ever realize the privilege that is ours when the Word of God comes to us? There is no greater miracle that can take place in a person's life because it always brings salvation.

A True Story for Our Times

Hundreds of times the Bible says that the Word of the Lord came to someone, and Jonah was a man whose life was changed by the experience. The Book of Jonah begins with the words, "Now the word of the Lord came to Jonah."

Many people find it hard to believe the account of Jonah, but I believe it is true—every bit of it. Jonah was the only prophet with whom Jesus personally identified. When the scribes and Pharisees asked Jesus to give them a sign, Jesus said,

> "An evil and adulterous generation seeks for a sign; but no sign shall be given to it except the sign of the prophet Jonah. For as Jonah was three days and three nights in the belly of the whale, so will the Son of Man be three days and three nights in the heart of the earth. The men of Nineveh will arise at the judgment with this generation and condemn it; for they repented at the preaching of Jonah, and behold, something greater than Jonah is here." (Mt 12:39-41)

The way Jesus compared his own impending death and resurrection to Jonah's experience in the belly of the whale is one of the things that convinces me of the authenticity of Jonah's account. Otherwise, what was the point of Jesus' comparison? It would be like me saying, "I have a giant blue ox just like Paul Bunyan's Babe." Since there was never a Babe, my claim would be discredited as imaginary, too.

The Book of Jonah is not a colorful myth that teaches a

nice moral lesson. It is a true account from which we can learn in detail.

Privileges Bring Responsibilities

Jonah's name means "dove." The dove is the symbol of the Holy Spirit, so it was fitting that a man privileged to be identified with the Holy Spirit of God also received a tremendous responsibility for conveying God's message. Privilege and responsibility always seem to go together.

We don't know much about Jonah before God spoke to him, except that he was a prophet from Galilee in the northern kingdom of Israel (see 2 Kings 14:25). On this occasion, God said that Jonah was to go to Nineveh and start proclaiming God's judgment on that city because its wickedness had become so great that God was going to destroy it in forty days.

Jonah was the first prophet recorded in Scripture to be sent as a missionary to a foreign country. Not only was it a foreign country but an enemy country as far as Israel was concerned. To say that he was reluctant is a bit of an understatement. What was his reaction? He ran—the other way!

Some of us ought to be able to understand his response, because we, too, are reluctant to go to Russia or China or Cuba or Nicaragua. Like Jonah, we think: "If I go, something might happen. People might repent. God might bless them, and then our enemies would be stronger." But God doesn't divide the world according to our geopolitical boundaries. When the Word of God comes, it moves our entire life into a different realm. We cannot compare the Kingdom of God with anything political.

On the contrary, if we would go into the land of the "adversary"—the Communist, the Muslim, the pagan— and effectively preach the gospel there, to our own surprise (and certainly to the whole world's advantage) we might soon find that they are not our "adversary" any longer.

Obedience, the Making of a Hero

Many of us think of Jonah as a failure, a runaway, or a disobedient prophet. But I say he was one of the greatest prophets, a real hero of the faith. Look at what he accomplished! He went to a very large, heathen city and conducted such an effective revival that everyone was converted, the judgment that God had pronounced upon the city was retracted, and the city survived.

It's true that initially Jonah was not only reluctant, but disobedient. But I have to ask myself, how often have I been reluctant to do the will of God? I'm not one who jumps at every occasion to serve God. Sometimes God has to drag me to the place where he wants me to be because it is not always my choice. Nineveh was not Jonah's choice, nor was Calvary Jesus' wish.

God uses various approaches with people to get them where they should be. Sometimes all he has to do is speak; sometimes he nudges them with circumstances. But sometimes he has to resort to catastrophe to get their attention, as he did in Jonah's case. But eventually Jonah became a great prophet with tremendous results.

We would like to imagine ourselves instantly responsive to God's still, small voice. But, as Jesus asked his disciples, which is better: to say we'll obey and then do nothing (or very little), or to rebel at first and then later repent and do all that our Master asks?

Passivity, the Unmaking of Any Hero

Possibly the only thing worse than running off in the wrong direction, as Jonah did, is not to move at all. Like a ship sitting becalmed in the water, when we are not moving, we are not easily steered. To the inactive church in Laodicea Christ had John write: "I know your works: you are neither cold nor hot. Would that you were cold or hot! So, because you are lukewarm, and neither cold nor hot, I will spew you out of my mouth" (Rv 3:15, 16). It is the passive do nothings God dislikes most. Surely the hottest seat must be preserved for those who knew about the problem and who knew about the solution, and then did nothing.

Jonah was anything but passive. He used God's money to pay for a Mediterranean cruise that didn't turn out as pleasant as the ad had promised. At that point Jonah was doing everything he could do to get away from the task God had for him. But God had another means of transportation planned because God still loved the world. He loved Nineveh, and he chose to send Jonah.

Make no mistake, when we speak about heroes of the faith, God doesn't pick out two or three good candidates hoping that one will respond. God calls a person. God calls you. He calls me. If we fail, he doesn't have a second string just waiting on the sidelines for a little time on the playing field. He has no second choices. Each person has his or her own call and responsibility. When Jonah failed to respond, God did not call Jonah Junior. God's call on Jonah remained the same, even when he was going the other way.

Meeting the Needs of the World

Jonah went to Joppa, the nearest seaport, found a ship headed for Tarsus, bought a one-way ticket, and got aboard. He went below deck and fell sound asleep. When God allowed a terrible storm to engulf the ship, Jonah slept on.

My mother used to say you can't sleep with a bad

conscience. But Jonah proved you can; even the storm didn't rouse him. The ship was breaking apart; the sailors were terrified. Yet Jonah slept right through the crisis. And we do the same. How dare we? The world is terrified, whole populations of children are malnourished, revolution is erupting, nuclear war threatens, yet we Christians dare to sleep.

When the sailors finally got Jonah awake, they said, "Tell us, on whose account this evil has come upon us? What is your occupation? And whence do you come? What is your country? And of what people are you?" (Jon 1:8). In the same way our angry world today demands that Christians speak out on what's really true. The world is not interested in a compromising message on the Bible, on creation and evolution, on liberal theology, on prosperity theology, on all those things that are only good for a few people. The world needs a message that's good for everybody. They need the message of the love of God. We as Christians have to realize that we can only become heroes of the faith when we declare the truth.

Integrity Always Gets a Hearing

If Jonah was going to proclaim the truth, however, he had to begin with a confession—that he was running away from God's commission. Many of us must begin at the same place. Only then will people accept the integrity of our message. It's interesting that when Jonah made his confession, the sailors immediately believed that he was, indeed, a messenger of God. What an effective start as a prophet! He overcame the hardest obstacle. The Bible says, "Then the men were exceedingly afraid, and said to him, 'What is this that you have done!' For the men knew that he was fleeing from the presence of the Lord, because he had told them" (Jon 1:10).

But Jonah wasn't ready yet to go to Nineveh. The

sailors asked, "What shall we do to you, that the sea may quiet down for us?" Jonah didn't say, "Turn the ship around and take me back to Joppa so I can fulfill God's call." Not Jonah; he'd rather die first. He said, "Throw me into the sea."

Guilt creates depression. Severe depression causes many people to despair of life and contemplate suicide. That was Jonah's condition. He knew the storm was his fault; he knew he had disobeyed God. He thought it was all over; he might as well die. But what he really needed was some quiet time, a chance to cool off and reflect on the character of God. And that's what he got . . . in the belly of the fish. Maybe to Jonah, who preferred to die rather than obey God, the thing that got his attention was the fact that God didn't let him die. It was a foretaste of the kind of mercy God was to later demonstrate to Nineveh.

Declaring God's Character

If we who serve the Lord knew more about the character of God, we would not become so easily discouraged. When we sin or make a mistake, we would not need to struggle under a burden of guilt and depression until we are ready to give up. To me one of the most important passages in the whole Bible is found in Exodus when the Lord, revealing his character to Moses, said, "[I am] the Lord, a God merciful and gracious, slow to anger, and abounding in steadfast love and faithfulness, keeping steadfast love for thousands, forgiving iniquity and transgression and sin . . ." (Ex 34:6, 7).

If we would memorize those verses and recall them in every circumstance—when we are lonely, depressed, attacked, criticized, misunderstood, or when we have sinned or feel we deserved God's anger—this statement of God's true character would carry us through and help us go on.

God's revelation of his nature should help us accept his forgiveness and believe that through our ministry God can indeed change other people and save not only our loved ones but our enemies. If we truly believed God, we would have aggressive evangelism to Russia without writing off "all those communists who hate God and burn Bibles and close the churches and imprison the pastors and exile the young people." We would begin to believe that God can make of Russia a more peace-loving country, one which we need not fear.

There in the belly of the fish Jonah began to pray. Chapter 2 records his prayer, and much of it is quoted Scripture, such as Psalms 120; 130; 42; 31; 69. God's "timeout" for Jonah worked. As he considered the character of God, his mind cleared, and he concluded by saying: "I with the voice of thanksgiving / will sacrifice to thee; / what I have vowed I will pay. / Deliverance belongs to the Lord!" (Jon 2:9).

Jonah was finally ready to go to Nineveh. The fish vomited him out on dry ground, God repeated his call, and this time Jonah "arose and went" (Jon 3:3).

If We Do Not Go, the Needy Will Come—As Our Enemy

Nineveh was a city in which every man, woman, boy, and girl was lost. Not just a little lost; they were facing utter annihilation. And Jonah was the one man who could save the city. But how could the man with the solution be brought together with the problem, a lost and condemned Nineveh? Only by obedience and taking the Word of God to those in need. Whatever God says, we must do. Whatever he speaks, we must repeat. We must give his message to the world. There was no other message that could save Nineveh, no other hope. Only Jonah held the key to their survival and their salvation. That's what made him a hero of the faith.

This is what we are really talking about when we speak about heroes of the faith—people who accept their responsibility to go to a lost world. I say "go" because that is what God said to Jonah and what Jesus said to us in Matthew 28, the Great Commission.

Nineveh—in fact, all of Assyria—was the enemy of Israel. God could have said, "Wait until they come to you." But how would they have come? As an occupying army, as soldiers, as invaders raping their women and girls and killing the men and taking away all their possessions. That's how they would have come.

It is still the same today. If we do not go to the heathen with the gospel, they will come to us. And we won't like the way they come. They'll come as terrorists; they'll come as criminals; they'll come as occupying armies. They will come to make war on us because we did not go to them. "Go," Jesus said, "go and proclaim."

The Fruit of Faithful Ministry

Obedience to God's "go and proclaim my Word" is what makes a prophet. That is what made the men and women of the Bible heroes of the faith. It was not because they themselves had such impressive characters. I don't think Jonah was a noble man. He does not appear to me to be a great person all by himself apart from the grace of God.

But the fact that God uses common people can give hope to you and me. Who am I? Who are you? And yet God's Word comes to us, and because that Word comes to us, suddenly we stand out. We become totally different people in a different situation. We know the answer! And the more we see crime, unrest, and lawlessness increase, the more we see the world's condition deteriorate, the more confident we ought to feel as Christians. Not because we enjoy seeing people in trouble, and certainly not because we'll go to Heaven and escape the trouble, but because if we obey and pay the price, people's lives will change.

Immediate Repentance

The most amazing thing happened when Jonah told the people of Nineveh that they had only forty days until the city would be overthrown: the people responded immediately. They did not wait thirty-nine days before they repented, enjoying their sin for as long as possible. Why? Jonah hadn't promised mercy. There was no certainty of a reprieve. The king of Nineveh said in his decree ordering repentance, "Who knows, God may yet repent and turn from his fierce anger, so that we perish not?" (Jon 3:9). I believe if they had taken the approach of trying to sin as long as possible, God's grace would not have come to them.

There is a story of a Jewish boy who came to visit his rabbi. The boy said, "Rabbi, when shall I repent?"

The Rabbi—a man of great wisdom—said, "Boy, you must repent one day before your death."

The boy got frightened and said, "I don't know when I will die."

"Exactly, son," the rabbi said. "So why not do it today?"

That is the answer. One doesn't trifle with a holy God.

Maintaining God's Perspective on the World

There is another aspect of this story that we could study at length, and that is Jonah's anger after Nineveh repented. However, I want to touch on only one aspect of it—the danger of success. When the people repented and God forgave them so that they were not destroyed, Jonah became very dejected and said, ". . . Lord, take my life from me, I beseech thee, for it is better for me to die than to live" (Jon 4:3). What can we learn from this?

On the boat when Jonah was under a great load of guilt, he had also become depressed and wanted to die. But God didn't let him die. In fact, in the belly of the fish, after getting right with the Lord, there was not a thought of suicide in Jonah's heart. His whole being craved to survive and to serve God. "What I have vowed I will pay," he boldly declared. But here, after his great success, he is again contemplating death. What made him despondent this time?

I think it is possible for success and affluence to cause people to lose God's perspective on life. Without God's perspective, it is easy to have a heavy heart with less motivation to do anything about the world than those who are persecuted. Why did Jonah have such a strong urge to get on with the job when he was confined in the belly of the fish? Exactly the same reason the church in China today is having a revival—their oppressed circumstances cause them to see the true condition of people without God. God's perspective on the world is sharpened in their hearts, and they find a strong reason to live. They are ready to proclaim Christ. We see the same happening in Rumania, Cuba, Nicaragua, Poland, East Germany, and the Soviet Union.

Once after I visited Corrie ten Boom in her home, she was saying good-bye to me. She shook my hand and said, "Andrew, keep looking down."

How strange, I thought. The usual encouragement is, "Keep looking up, friend."

Corrie noticed the confusion on my face, and explained, "Yes, Andrew, keep looking down. Look at the world from God's perspective, and you'll see something so different."

I was reminded of the importance of this perspective on life some time ago when I met a Russian-speaking American evangelist after he had returned from Russia. I also had just returned from there, having delivered a big load of Russian Bibles. "Andrew," he said, "you've got to stop bringing Bibles to Russia because there is a pastor who's been selling the Bibles for eighty rubles apiece" (about two weeks' salary for the average worker).

This was certainly an unfortunate situation because we gave those Bibles free to be distributed free. But I said to him, "Brother, your observation is correct. But your conclusion is wrong. Rather than stop delivering Bibles, we've got to bring more Bibles to Russia so that the price goes down." You see, the one response continued the work while the other would have stopped it. We observed the same conditions, but different perspectives led to different conclusions.

In order to be heroes of the faith, we must keep God's perspective in mind. Maybe you've been reluctant to proclaim God's Word when God told you to. Maybe you turned and ran the other way, and now you feel you've lost your chance. But the Ninevehs of the world are still lost; they are still waiting for our obedience. If we learn from Jonah, and what happened when he finally overcame his reluctance (with a little help from God Almighty), we'll have plenty of encouragement for turning around and heeding God's call. The lives of real people are at stake.

SIX

Daniel: A Hero for Hostile Times

WHILE PREACHING IN A COMMUNIST COUNTRY several years ago, I talked with my interpreter about how far we should go in defying various government restrictions on the proclamation of the gospel. We had been pretty bold, getting in trouble occasionally. We were arrested and thrown out of the country, only to get another passport and go back in, where we got arrested again.

My friend—who is still in Eastern Europe—said, "Andrew, I want you to think a little more about Daniel. When Daniel was in the lions' den, God did protect him, but he did not go around pulling the lions' tails. Nor did he try to brush their teeth."

How far can we go in the face of danger? How far can we defy the enemy? To what degree should we stand up and proclaim that Jesus Christ is Lord?

It is easy to shout "hallelujah" when you know there will be a lot of "amens" coming from your audience. But who among us is going to stand up in Red Square or in a public place in another society that is antagonistic to Christianity and shout "hallelujah?" Who is going to make such a hostile setting his or her platform to tell people that God is love? In situations where the political system or the prevailing religion is determined to wipe out the church, where the forces in power have become a direct instrument of the devil, who will stand up and single-handedly—if need be—proclaim that Jesus Christ is Lord? Who will tell the people that the Word of God is true, and that the devil is not going to have his way?

I think Daniel was such a man! And that's just as dangerous as pulling the tail of a lion.

The Components of Crisis

Daniel lived during one of those low tides in Israel's history when everything had gone wrong. Jerusalem had been destroyed, the temple was in ruins, the leaders had been killed, and the youths taken off to Babylon in exile— Daniel and his friends among them.

Satan, the inspiration behind Israel's enemies, was making an all-out attempt to eradicate the Jewish people as a nation, but his deeper goal was to destroy the plan God had for the redemption of humanity. That purpose is always behind Satan's attacks. In a way, you could say the devil is not against individual people; he is against our willingness to do God's will. That's why some people who do not believe seem to have a much easier life than those who do believe. Satan does not oppose them.

The writer of Psalm 73 wondered the same thing: "I was envious of the arrogant, / when I saw the prosperity of the wicked. / . . . always at ease, they increase in riches. / All in vain have I kept my heart clean / and washed my hands in innocence. / For all the day long I have been stricken, / and chastened every morning" (Ps 73:3, 12-14). But then the psalmist took a look at how their life ended (after all, it is the end that counts), for he said: "But when I thought how to understand this, / it seemed to me a wearisome task, / until I went into the sanctuary of God; / then I perceived their end. / Truly thou dost set them in slippery places; / thou dost make them fall in ruin" (Ps 73:16-18). The end is determined by the beginning.

Attack on the Identity of the Faithful

When the captives arrived in Babylon, King Nebuchadnezzar's chief eunuch assigned new names to the Hebrew young men (see Daniel 1:7). This was because their Jewish names were related to their destiny as appointed by God Almighty. The enemy was not satisfied with moving the Hebrews out of their own country so that Jerusalem could not function. He wanted to destroy their identity.

Satan's objective was to make sure the messianic prophecies could never come true. If there was no nation, no identifiable people who could return and rebuild a nation, there would be no Jesus born in Bethlehem. If there was no Jesus, there would be no Savior of the Hebrew people and of all the world who would be crucified in Jerusalem and rise again according to all the prophecies.

Not only did the devil want to destroy all God's plans, he also wanted to eradicate all the religious remains. By taking away the captives' names and giving them heathen names—occult names of heathen gods—their whole religion was in jeopardy. There was a good chance that they would completely forget the God of their fathers.

The Durability of True Faith

But apparently Daniel didn't allow his new name to stick. It's amusing that Scripture says, "Daniel continued until the first year of King Cyrus" (Dn 1:21). Cyrus was the *fourth* king in succession after Nebuchadnezzar, and still he was being called Daniel. Belteshazzar, the name the king's eunuch assigned, never replaced it.

That delights me! It means the devil cannot succeed in eradicating true faith in God. It will always be there. Evil people come and go, but God's people will remain. This is encouraging because in today's world, with constant threats of revolution and active persecution spreading to more and more countries, it's easy to fear that soon the church may be completely wiped out. But change the believers' names and give them numbers instead, drive them from their homeland, take away Sunday for worship, take away the Bible, take away their freedom, even take away the liberty that Christian parents should have to teach the Word of God to their own children, and the church will still survive. Jesus has promised: ". . . I will build my church, and the powers of death shall not prevail against it" (Mt 16:18).

Although Daniel was brought to Babylon as a captive, King Nebuchadnezzar selected a group of bright young men—Daniel and three of his friends among them—to be trained and groomed for special service to the king. What a ripe situation for temptation! Cut off from their home and religious heritage, prisoners in a strange land, yet indulged, educated, favored, flattered. Many young people would say, "Oh, well, why fight it; this is a pretty good deal," and embrace the idolatry of this new life.

Daniel and his three friends, however, refused to go along with the lifestyle of the king's court. They did not want to defile themselves with the rich food and wines normally on the menu for young men being trained to serve the king. The amazing thing is that they refused in such a way that they were allowed to follow their religious beliefs in this matter, and when the king saw the results, he commended them for it.

This was just the beginning of trying to be heroes of the faith in a hostile land. One day Hananiah (Shadrach), Mishael (Meshach), and Azariah (Abednego) were governors over the province; the next they were thrown into a fiery furnace for refusing to worship the image of the king. One day Daniel was the king's most trusted advisor; the next he was in the lions' den because his colleagues had plotted against him. But whether they were honored or persecuted, they remained steadfast in their belief in the one true God and their identity as his children. And all the Babylonian kings, from Nebuchadnezzar to Cyrus, were deeply affected by the steadfastness of their faith and the truth of the words they spoke.

The Frailty of the Godless

In contrast to the durability of the faithful, the story of Daniel also shows us the frailty of the godless. In Daniel 2:1 we read that King Nebuchadnezzar was having bad dreams, his spirit was troubled, and his sleep left him. Isn't that unusual? The king of the strongest empire in the world trembled because of one thing he couldn't explain. Something supernatural was happening, and the whole empire shook to its very foundations. It shows the weakness of the godless.

According to the communists' plan in our own century, after sixty to seventy years of revolution there shouldn't be a church left in Russia. But what's happening today? A revival, and they can't stop it. It shakes them; they don't know how to handle it. The late chairman Mao thought that after ten or fifteen years—certainly after the cultural revolution from 1965 to 1975—there should be no church left at all in China. But the communist leaders are awakening from their dream. They see that the church is ten or twenty or fifty times bigger than it ever was. They cannot explain it.

These amazing things give us great joy as we travel in the countries where Christians have been persecuted. We are not fighting a lost cause. We are winning! These antagonistic regimes tremble because things are happening there that they cannot explain. In Russia, parents still take their children to be baptized. In Eastern Europe, young people come to the Lord. In Nicaragua, the church has grown three times since the Sandinistas took over. The oppressors don't know what is happening. What a tremendous perspective for us today as we fight this spiritual war.

The Nature of the Conflict

Daniel was able to interpret Nebuchadnezzar's dream, and even though the interpretation was a strong warning and judgment against the king, Daniel won the king's respect and became an esteemed ruler in the land. Later, during the reign of Belshazzar, Daniel also had a dream. Part of the interpretation explained the tactics that the enemy uses against God and his people: "He shall speak words against the Most High, / and shall wear out the saints of the Most High, / and shall think to change the times and the law . . ." (Dn 7:25).

The battle described here is a battle of words, of ideas and ideologies. It involves attacks on what we believe. It is a battle for the mind, and that is why we must never give up our vision of the Kingdom of God. We must remember our commission from Jesus to preach the gospel to the whole world and make disciples of every nation. Until all peoples know about God and worship him voluntarily, there will always be this battle. Evil will always fight good; darkness will always oppose light; hatred will always try to replace love. The devil will always try to unseat Jesus Christ from his throne in our hearts, from his throne in society and over the whole world. Not everyone knows that all the kingdoms of the world will one day become the kingdoms of Christ Jesus our Lord.

One of the devil's most effective tactics is propaganda deluge. He speaks out. He will talk, talk, talk just like the giant Goliath. Goliath made the same boastful claim for forty days, every morning and every night. That means eighty times he brought the same evil, atheistic, nihilistic, anarchistic sermon: "You will never do it; you won't make it; you'll always be slaves; you'll always be weak; you'll always be defeated; you'll never have the victory." No matter how false or outrageous the message, the human mind tends to succumb to that kind of barrage. Daniel said that the evil one intends to "wear out the saints" speaking words against the Most High.

The Response of a Hero

I see this happening in the world today. We in the church are getting so tired of the unrelenting propaganda from every side, both the left and the right, that we are ready to throw up our hands in despair of ever sorting out the truth. But God has an answer!

Know your God. Daniel 11:32 says that the evil one "shall seduce with flattery those who violate the covenant; but the people who know their God shall stand firm and take action." There is victory for the people who know their God, but knowing takes time. You can never get to know any person unless you spend time with that person. Our problem is that we are not feeding ourselves enough on the Word of God for us to get to know him. No wonder we lack peace, security, and joy. We are being worn out. I want to warn you not to become worn out by what you hear. Spend less time reading books that do not matter, less time watching television. It's just like marriage; the more time you spend with your partner, the better life becomes.

Stand firm. God's people who know him will display

strength. Our strength is from the Holy Spirit, but it is also the strength of our character, the strength of our "guts," our moral courage to stand up in the face of evil.

Take action. Daniel 11:33 says, "And those among the people who are wise shall make many understand." This is the action we are to take. We are to denounce evil, expose it, and proclaim that Jesus Christ is Lord. We will not let God's people be persecuted until they no longer know what to do.

To be effective in bringing understanding to people, however, we've got to have insight into the problems that exist today, exactly as they existed in the time of Daniel. That is why we must learn from these heroes of the faith.

Prayer in a Crisis

Even in the darkest hour, God will not forget a people as long as there is even one person who qualifies in the sight of God to be a hero of faith, who can claim his nation back for God. What happened to God's people in Babylon?

Daniel 9:2 records events in the first year of Darius' reign: "I, Daniel, perceived in the books the numbers of years which, according to the word of the Lord to Jeremiah the prophet, must pass before the end of the desolations of Jerusalem, namely, seventy years." By this time Daniel was already in his nineties. He had stood by his three friends as they went through the experience of the fiery furnace. He had survived persecution in the lions' den. He had had many confrontations with the ways the Babylonians wanted to subvert the Hebrews, both on the grounds of their religion and their distinctiveness as a people. But always God's people came out as winners because there were heroes willing to lay down their lives for the truth—and even the pagan kings respected them for it.

Searching for God's Plan

On a quiet morning, Daniel turned to the Book of Jeremiah and read:

> For thus says the Lord: When seventy years are completed for Babylon, I will visit you, and I will fulfill to you my promise and bring you back to this place. For I know the plans I have for you, says the Lord, plans for welfare and not for evil, to give you a future and a hope. Then you will call upon me and come and pray to me, and I will hear you. You will seek me and find me; when you seek me with all your heart, I will be found by you.... (Jer 29:10-14)

Who was going to be that hero to search for God with all his heart? Daniel. He was the only one who did any searching at all, and he discovered in the book the prediction that the captivity would end after seventy years. Then he looked at the calendar and saw that the time was up. That year something big was going to happen. God had a plan: "We're going to get out of this place!"

But were they? Here is the secret of intercession. You may say, "Well, the prophecy said the captivity was going to be over." That's true; it *was* the appointed time. But the prophecy also said, "Then you will call upon me and come and pray to me." There was more to it than an automatic, guaranteed deliverance. God interacts with us. Remember that Nineveh was not destroyed simply because there had been a prophecy to that effect. The people's response affected the outcome.

Praying According to God's Plan

Situations can be changed when God "changes his mind" because somebody steps into the gap and does something about it, fulfilling the conditions God has set forth. What did Daniel do? When Daniel saw that it was the appointed year, he did not close his Bible, fold his arms across his chest and say, "Well, praise the Lord, now the end is near." No. I personally think that Israel might not have gotten out of exile at that particular time had not Daniel reacted the way he did.

He read what God said through Jeremiah, and then he did something very dramatic. He called upon the name of the Lord because he knew that even though the prophecy was written in the book, it would still have to happen through people who would get involved in a personal way to make deliverance happen. Therefore he said, "I prayed to the Lord my God and made confession" (Dn 9:4). In this mighty prayer of confession, he worshiped God, the great and awesome God who keeps covenants and is steadfast in loving kindness for those who love him and keep his commands.

Then Daniel admitted the condition of his people, confessing their sin—not just a few little mistakes, but ". . . we have sinned and done wrong and acted wickedly and rebelled, turning aside from thy commandments and ordinances; we have not listened to thy servants . . ." (Dn 9:5, 6). In all this Daniel indentified with the people, yet when we study the life of Daniel it appears that he is just about the only person (other than Jesus) of whom nothing negative is mentioned anywhere in Scripture. He was a mighty warrior for God, but he got on his knees in sackcloth and ashes, humbling himself to identify with his people.

After confessing the sin and praising the Lord, Daniel said,

> O my God, incline thy ear and hear; . . . for we do not present our supplications before thee on the ground of our righteousness, but on the ground of thy great

mercy. O Lord, hear; O Lord, forgive; O Lord, give heed and act; delay not, for thy own sake, O my God, because thy city and thy people are called by thy name. (Dn 9:18-19)

To me this is most reassuring. We have a basis for our intercession for the suffering church in Russia and China. We have a basis for our prayer that God will help us to break open all those doors and borders and barriers—not because we deserve to have our prayers answered, but because of God's great mercy and because those people are called by his name.

Praying as a Participant in God's Plan

Would the Hebrews have gone back to Jerusalem had Daniel not prayed? That's the wrong question. In God's economy, those who remind God of his characteristic mercy and forgiveness, who humble themselves, who confess their sin and the sin of the nation, are used by God to bring about his word. The question should be: Where are the heroes of the faith who will participate in God's plan through prayer?

God's promises are not something that are detached from human affairs. Even though God said it, God still needs people to make it happen. That is really the whole process of becoming heroes of the faith. That is what makes people Christlike—when they say, like Jesus, "I came to do thy will, O God."

God works through people. God worked mightily through Daniel. We see him battle through in prayer; we see him fight the paralysis that came upon his nation because they were worn out and worn down by the enemy and his relentless propaganda.

But then came that tremendous day not long after this prayer when Daniel stood at the gates of Babylon and saw the first group of Hebrews return to Jerusalem to rebuild the temple and the city, and eventually the walls themselves, so that the people could live and worship God in peace and safety.

How do we measure up when the society around us tries to seduce us with an indulgent lifestyle, with all the "knowledge" of a secular education, with privileged positions? Yet all of us who are children of the Most High God are strangers in a strange land, no matter where we live. Even in our own country, where we experience great freedom in religious matters, we also face hostile forces whose desire is to wipe out godly influences from political, social, educational, and even family life.

Will we, as Daniel and his friends, stand firmly as heroes of the faith, whether we are honored or persecuted for our action? Will we be steadfast, even though the enemy tries to wear us down with constant godless propaganda? Will we be faithful to confess our sins and the sins of our people, and pray for God's will to be done in the land?

God calls each of us to be a Daniel in our own time.

SEVEN

Nehemiah: Asking the Right Questions

I N 1955 I WAS INVITED TO ATTEND a youth festival in Warsaw, Poland. About 30,000 foreigners had flocked into the country to see for themselves how the communists had rebuilt Warsaw after the World War II devastation of the Nazis. I went to try and make contact with the Polish Christians.

Almost everyone I spoke to was very impressed with this "workers' paradise" as they went on guided tours of the new schools, factories, and high-rise apartments. Hans, a communist from Amsterdam, told me one day how enthusiastic he was about what he had seen and heard. He couldn't understand why I was not.

"Why don't you skip tomorrow's guided tour and take a little walk on your own?" I asked. Then I suggested that he follow a route I had found that within a few short blocks would get him behind the facade and dump him into the rubble and bombed-out basements in which thousands still lived. "Talk to some of those people," I suggested, "and see what they think of the progress."

To his credit, he went and asked his questions. And that evening when I saw Hans, he looked pale and frightened. "Andrew," he said, "I'm leaving tonight on the midnight train. I'm scared stiff by what I've seen and heard today."

The value of being nosy and asking the right questions can turn up some disturbing conditions in any modern city. For instance, if you leave JFK Airport in New York and head into the Bronx, you might encounter circumstances that would cause you either to run away or to get involved in ministry to those needs as David Wilkerson did with Teen Challenge. The same is true in Calcutta, London, or Amsterdam.

Having to face reality may cause many to run. Indeed, aspiring to change the world when we've seen its sad reality may seem far too grandiose for the average person, and that's as it should be if we are operating in our own strength. Anyone who thinks otherwise has delusions of grandeur. However, God uses ordinary people who are willing to ask those hard questions about how things really are.

There's someone in Scripture who illustrates this very clearly: Nehemiah. In my opinion, the Bible is a book about ordinary people who became extraordinary by asking the right questions and then by letting God into their lives. This change from ordinary to extraordinary comes to pass at the moment when we respond to the call of God. And that call of God comes to you.

The Call of an Ordinary Man

Let's look at the life of a fairly average man, Nehemiah. The Book of Nehemiah is the story of a nation in exile. Its message is very up-to-date because today's world has more refugees than ever before. According to statistics provided by the United States Committee for Refugees, figures soared by more than one and a quarter million in 1986. The year ended with 11,698,000 refugees in the world—4.7 million from Afghanistan, 3.1 million in Africa, 2.1 million Palestinians, a million in Southeast Asia, and over a quarter of a million from Central

America—to list the world's worst trouble spots. (Statistics are from the *World Refugee Survey, 1986 in Review,* April 1987.)

The whole United States was really founded by the inflow of refugees and immigrants. Many who came were forced to do so by persecution, lack of liberty, or because of desperate need. In the world today, this is a greater problem than ever before.

Twenty-six centuries ago, Israel was in exile. We don't have to study much to find out why. Every time things really went wrong for Israel, it was because of sin. God's power and love are great enough to protect people who walk according to his will and precepts, but the Book of Nehemiah opens with God's people far away from where they should or could have lived:

> The words of Nehemiah the son of Hacaliah.
> Now it happened in the month of Chislev, in the twentieth year, as I was in Susa the capital, that Hanani, one of my brethren, came with certain men out of Judah; and I asked them concerning the Jews that survived, who had escaped exile, and concerning Jerusalem. And they said to me, "The survivors there in the province who escaped exile are in great trouble and shame; the wall of Jerusalem is broken down, and its gates are destroyed by fire." (Neh 1:1-3)

Ordinary People in a World at War

From the very first pages of the Bible, we find that God and Satan are involved in the ultimate holy war over the souls of men and women. Satan seems to have taken the first round by seducing the human race into sin, but God set in motion a counterattack—a plan for the redemption of all men and women.

Of course the devil fought back. God had already

provided for the problem of sin. But Satan tried to destroy God's plan even though the Bible says that the Lamb, Jesus Christ, was "slain from the foundation of the world" (Rv 13:8 KJV). All that was needed was time to fulfill God's plan, and people—heroes of the faith—to carry out his purposes.

Every effort of Satan's which is recorded throughout the Old Testament was an attempt to disrupt that plan. Of particular intensity were his attempts to prevent Jesus from being born in Bethlehem. Satan failed to prevent Christ's birth or to obstruct his ministry, particularly his redemptive sacrifice on the cross, so his total attentions today are focused on discrediting the Body of Christ and hindering the spread of the gospel. If you remember these underlying objectives of Satan's as you study the Bible and observe world events, you will gain a great deal of insight and understanding into what has happened and really is happening. It will give you a new perspective as you see how God has called people, sometimes at great personal cost, to thwart the purposes of Satan.

Nehemiah's Comfort Disrupted

If we consider Nehemiah in the context of this cosmic struggle, we will gain a new appreciation for him as a hero of the faith. He enjoyed quite a comfortable life. Nehemiah lived in Susa, the capital of Persia or present-day Iran. As far as we know, he had no major personal problems. It's true that he still lived in exile himself, but the conditions were pleasant—at least a lot better than back home in Judah. He had a good job as the cupbearer to the king (cf. Neh 2:1). It was a terrific job—palatial working environment, fantastic fringe benefits, tremendous prestige. What else could he want?

Then one day Nehemiah met someone who had just come from Judah, and he asked him two questions: "How are those who escaped being exiled?" and "What has happened to Jerusalem, our beloved city?" Because of those two questions, Nehemiah was never the same again.

Ask and You Will Learn

I guarantee that, like Nehemiah, if you ask the right questions, you will never be the same again. Several years ago the director of our Open Doors ministry in Asia asked the right question when he met some Chinese believers. The result was millions of Bibles sent into China—one million in a single nighttime beach landing. He didn't ask, "How are the living conditions? Do you need food? Do you need medicine or money?" He didn't ask about the remnants of any pre-war mission agency or even whether the people needed Bibles. What he asked was, "How is the Body of Christ?"

That question gave those believers from China such confidence in our ministry that they risked accepting our help. Because they opened up as individual believers, all of China opened up to our ministry. All this was because our director asked the right question.

Ask about the Suffering Church

"How are the Jews doing that survived the captivity?" Nehemiah asked. He was asking about the suffering church.

Over thirty years ago God told me to "strengthen what remains." To what was he referring? The remains after the captivity, the remains after the exile, the remains after the persecution, the remains after the Holocaust, the remains after all the massacres, the remains after all that has taken place where the devil has tried to annihilate the church of Jesus Christ.

Recently when such terrible famine was ravaging

Ethiopia, were we asking the right questions? In one province in Ethiopia the government closed 748 churches in a two-month period. But no one mentioned that. You didn't see it in your newspaper or on TV. We were overwhelmed by the shocking reports of all those dying children, and well we should have been. But who was asking about God's people? Did we ask the questions that could make a strategic difference in the future of that nation? Did we ask questions that elevated us above the level of being exploited to do no more than give handouts to people? Don't we believe that if Ethiopia is going to return to health as a country, the church will have to play a vital role? Is the economic and military power of Western governments the only way we can imagine to rescue a country like Ethiopia from the cruel grip of Marxism which organizes mass famines to subdue its tribes?

Ask about the Strategic Opportunities

"How are those who escaped being exiled?" and "What has happened to Jerusalem, our beloved city?" I think those were the right questions for Nehemiah to ask. One was people oriented, and the other was strategy oriented. Both had God's plan for his people at heart.

God had promised a Messiah. But before he could come there had to be a people to receive him and a place for his mission. There had to be a family, a lineage, a heritage. There had to be a people who knew God so that some, at least, would welcome him as the Messiah. One day he would go to the temple—the same temple that had been destroyed by Babylon. One day he would teach the descendants of those who had been scattered in exile and gathered again. One day he would die on a cross and rise from the borrowed tomb of a rich man. There had to be a place.

God has always called upon people to carry out his

plan, no matter what the devil tries to do to stop it. This should make us feel good even in the midst of great conflict. If God has enough confidence in you to call you to participate in his plan, then you qualify to be a hero of the faith. The only requirement is that you decide to do the will of God.

Response to the Information

It has been said many times that pastors only answer questions that no one is asking. But I think it is worse. I think people are not asking questions any more, at least not with an openness to receiving and acting upon the answers. We need to ask what we can do, and we need to be ready to respond to the answer.

For instance, why was the apostle Paul so successful? There are many reasons, but one of them was his propensity to action. He was a fighter. Before his conversion he was even fighting against Jesus. That's why Jesus took such a special interest in him. He knew that when Paul understood that he had been resisting God, his conversion would redirect him to fight *for* the gospel. Paul used the metaphor of being a captive to Jesus Christ. How can you ever be a captive if you are not conscious of having been part of the opposition?

Identifying the Specific Problem

When Nehemiah asked about the condition of Jerusalem, he was told that the wall was broken down and that its gates were destroyed by fire. What was the significance of this report, other than the fact that things were in great disrepair? It basically described one problem: there was no protection for the people. And if the people were not protected, there was no way they could really live the life of God. The psalmist said, "If the

foundations are destroyed, / what can the righteous do?"
(Ps 11:3). This suggests that even God's people can do
nothing if there is no protection.

That protection does not necessarily or fundamentally
come from the government, even in a free country. It is
not a protection that automatically comes just by being a
child of God. It is important to realize that the temple had
already been rebuilt at this time. But even with the temple,
the focus of religious practice, life was very tenuous
because *community*—standing together as a people—was
not possible without the protection of a wall.

We have churches everywhere and believers who
frequent them often. But we'll only have the protection
that fosters the dynamic life of God when we repair the
wall of Christian community—the caring and unity that
should characterize the Body of Christ.

Grasping the Immensity of the Need

Nehemiah was determined to be a vital part of God's
people. When he got the word that his people were in
great distress and reproach, something happened within
him. He could have said, "It's too far from my bed; I'll
probably never get there anyway. I've taken pretty good
care of myself; my future is secure; my pension is all
settled, and I live a good life. No one can blame me." But
he did not do that. He did what every hero of faith should
do and will do when we grasp the immensity of the need.
This is what happened:

> When I heard these words I sat down and wept, and
> mourned for days; and I continued fasting and praying
> before the God of heaven. And I said, "O Lord God of
> heaven, the great and terrible God who keeps covenant
> and steadfast love with those who love him and keep his
> commandments; let thy ear be attentive, and thy eyes

open, to hear the prayer of thy servant which I now pray
before thee day and night for the people of Israel. . . ."
(Neh 1:4-6)

If we really want to become heroes of the faith, if we
want to be men and women of God, we cannot have any
other reaction than great grief when we hear that our
brothers and sisters in Christ around the world are in
great distress.

Do you know there is a law in Russia that forbids
Christian parents from giving their own children a
Christian education? That's an example of stripping
God's people of their protection. In Russia, as father and
mother you cannot legally teach your own children to
pray and love Jesus and believe the Bible. It's forbidden.

A church I visited in the Soviet Union told me they had
lost their pastor because he had made a terrible mistake.
During a Christmas service he had turned to some of the
younger people in the church and said, "Children, do you
know why Jesus came into the world?" That was his
Christmas sermon. For that one question he was thrown
out of the church and exiled to a lonely place where there
was no church and no fellowship.

We are in a world where 66 percent of the population
lives in restricted areas without the liberty that we know.
Why? Have they sinned? There is a terrible, terrible
theory—and I hate it with my whole being—which says
that if you're suffering it must be because you've sinned. It
claims that if you keep God's law, pay your tithes, and do
this or that, you'll have no problems. I hate that theory
because it is an insult to the suffering church, the
brothers and sisters who are on the front line paying the
price in this cosmic battle between God and Satan.

God is working out his purpose with his children. I'm
convinced that those who are in concentration camps for
their faith today are there because they are paying the

price for *my* liberty, for *your* liberty. What an ungrateful insult to suggest that they are paying for their own wrongdoing.

There is a suffering church today. A greater part of the church is suffering than ever before, and what are we doing? Our Open Doors mission keeps track of Christian prisoners in the Soviet Union. We have names and pictures of hundreds of Christian leaders who are in prison in Russia today. Some have very large families, ten or fifteen children. I feel like Nehemiah when I hear about them. I sit down and cry, but I must do more.

Confession Begins at Home

Nehemiah's next response is a touching prayer of confession, not on behalf of those who are persecuted, as though their plight was their fault, but on behalf of *himself and his family,* living in comfort and ease.

> . . . we have sinned against thee. Yea, I and my father's house have sinned. We have acted very corruptly against thee, and have not kept the commandments, the statutes, and the ordinances which thou didst command thy servant Moses. (Neh 1:6, 7)

It is because *we* have not kept God's commandments that there is so much need in the world. I am convinced that our sins of *omission* are far greater than our sins of commission. We can behave politely, morally, even religiously, and yet never do anything valuable for Jesus.

Many of us have never even bothered to do the will of God. But all of that can change by asking the right question: "How are my brethren doing?" This question made Nehemiah into an instrument of God, and it can do the same for you.

Ready for Action

It was with this preparation—having asked the right questions, having grasped the enormity of the need, and having made a confession of past sin—that Nehemiah was prepared for action. God blessed his actions mightily, too. He received the king's full cooperation and assistance as well as God's blessing when he returned to Jerusalem. The mission was blessed, but it was not easy.

During the rebuilding of the walls, Nehemiah suffered mocking taunts, plots to disrupt the work, attacks from enemies, false rumors spread about his motives, and threats against his life. Yet in the midst of all these obstacles, Nehemiah did not lose sight of the vision to complete his task.

I have a friend who asked many questions about Siberia. He knew that the Lord was calling him to be a missionary in that bleak corner of the earth, but how could it come about?

"The only way you can become a missionary to Siberia," he was told by a Russian Christian, "is to get arrested in Russia, and then you will be sent there."

What an answer to his question! What was his response? He did just that and spent twenty-four years in Siberian prison camps living under terrible conditions. There was a great deal of violence, murder, and forced labor in sub-zero temperatures. But every day, during that whole time, he was a missionary for Jesus, sharing his faith with others in the camps. Many came to know Christ through his unselfish ministry.

When he was finally released (he was exchanged for two Russian spies who were caught in New York), I met him. "Andrew," he said, "Not once during those twenty-four years was I sick, not even for a day. God kept his hand on me during the whole time."

God keeps his hand on all those who, after asking the right questions, are willing to pay the price. Are you asking the right questions? Are you willing to pay the price?

EIGHT

Paul: The Apostle of Confrontation

I WAS VISITING A HAVANA HOSPITAL, and written on the wall of the big reception room was a quotation from Che Guevara, a hero of the Cuban revolution: "If this revolution isn't aimed at changing people, then I am not interested."

In Christ, we are called to a similar revolution, but one based on love, which provides the courage to follow him and face the life of conflict and confrontation that is part of real Christianity.

No one illustrates this courage more than Paul, the "apostle of confrontation." He spoke constantly of the spiritual warfare in which Christians engage, never fearing to clash with the powers about him. At the same time, he was an apostle of love and a man of deep emotions, a living example of how "God's love has been poured into our hearts" (Rom 5:5). It was from this love that Paul had the courage to confront.

He knew firsthand what Christians were up against because at one time he had personified the other side of the conflict. This was the same Saul, a rigorous student of the law, who had stood by approvingly while an angry crowd stoned Stephen the deacon. Stephen's death sparked a great persecution against the Christians, and

"Saul was ravaging the church, and entering house after house, he dragged off men and women and committed them to prison" (Acts 8:3). When he himself became a believer—confronted by the voice of Jesus while on the road to Damascus "still breathing threats and murder against the disciples of the Lord" (Acts 9:1)—Saul became Paul, and where he had once confronted the truth of God with fanatical religious tradition, he now confronted the lies of Satan with the truth that had redeemed his life. It took courage, but Paul was certain of the foundation on which he stood.

The Courage to Confront

One of the hallmarks of courageous people, however, is that they are not conscious of their courage. It's just a part of their lives; otherwise, they would be actors. Courage is what other people see you have, not something you claim for yourself.

What was the focus of Paul's courage? It was Jesus. "Be imitators of me, as I am of Christ," Paul told his flock (1 Cor 11:1). What a testimony! His whole life was concentrated on being so close to Jesus that God's love filled his heart and enabled him to accomplish things he would never have done otherwise. It was just a natural part of him.

Don't think it is anything special when you stoop down into the gutter to pick people up or when you penetrate the Iron Curtain to minister in spite of threats from the authorities. That's not your innate courage; it's just the strength that comes from following the Holy Spirit as Paul did.

I picture Paul as a real "he-man," a fighter. This wasn't something that began when he became an apostle, either. He had persecuted the church with great enthusiasm, hounding Christians from Jerusalem to Damascus in his zeal. But when Paul met Jesus on the road to Damascus and surrendered his life to him (cf. Acts 9), his whole background and personality were redirected into proper channels, just as our earlier experiences can be used by God, no matter how ungodly they were.

In the Book of Acts we see Paul almost enjoying the uproar he caused wherever he went. The more people went after him, the more he seemed to revel in the controversy. He knew that if the Word of God is at work, it will challenge the *status quo* and kick up a fuss. This was something he just came to expect.

For example, early in his ministry he returned to Damascus to preach the gospel. After a while, the Jewish leaders couldn't stand it any more and plotted to kill him. His followers had to sneak him out of the city by lowering him down the wall in a basket at night (Acts 9:19-25). Paul seemed unaffected by this, not even fearing the angry mob.

Yet this same Paul told the elders from Ephesus that he had not ceased "night or day to admonish every one with tears" (Acts 20:31). Think of it: one of the strongest men in the New Testament, weeping because of compassion for the lost. Just as Jesus wept at the tomb of Lazarus because of the people's unbelief, Paul shed tears over the idolatry he saw throughout the Greek and Roman world.

The Reason to Confront

Righteous anger mixed with compassion—that's the key to understanding Paul. It isn't hard to become angry; many people become angry when they have to stop at a red light. Paul's anger, on the other hand, was motivated by his love. For example, in his letter to the church in Rome he said, "I could wish that I myself were accursed and cut off from Christ for the sake of my brethren, my kinsmen by race. They are Israelites . . ." (Rom 9:3). How many of us who travel as "holy tourists" to Israel would say this? If that same compassion burned in our hearts, even to the point of giving up our own salvation if it would mean the salvation of others, then Israel would not be the same today . . . nor would the church.

Whether free or in jail, Paul's only desire was to be used by God. Even when they put him in the prison cell at Philippi, he spent the time singing to the glory of God. How could he be so strong in the face of adversity? Perhaps we can find the answer back on the Damascus Road.

The Right to Confront

When Paul first met Jesus face to face, he asked the Lord what he should do. In reply, God told him instead how much he would suffer. In other words, God showed him what he had to *be*, not what he had to *do*.

Often, we try to *do* things for God rather than *be* what he wants us to be. We must have consistency of character in order to have the right to confront. Without the *being*, the *doing* is inconsistent. God showed Paul that there was a price to pay for the power to change the world, and that price was the willingness to allow his character to be transformed.

In Acts 17 we learn that Paul had the custom of going to the synagogue whenever he arrived in a city. There, he presented evidence from the Scriptures that the Messiah had to suffer, die, and rise again—a scenario that did not fit the Jews' expectations. This was a powerful confrontation because by demonstrating that the Messiah did have to suffer, Paul justified the Christian claim that Jesus was that very Messiah they were looking for.

In many ways Paul earned the right to confront by starting where the people were: waiting, waiting for the Messiah. He used the very Scriptures they were familiar with; he identified with them. He was a Jew; he had studied the Scriptures; he had kept the law. He earned the right to be heard.

The Consequences of Confrontation

Yet the arrival of Paul and his group of evangelists in a city often caused panic. He didn't ask for the red carpet treatment or a delegation from the mayor. All he wanted was a simple hearing of his message. The reaction, however, was often vicious.

It was obvious then, as it is now, that something was wrong in the world, and God wanted to make it right through Jesus Christ. But the Jewish leaders, who hated the Romans more than anything in the world, suddenly turned into Roman loyalists and loudly complained that Paul was trying to proclaim another king besides Caesar!

This was a dangerous accusation, but, in fact, it happened to be true. Paul taught the people to go against the decrees of Caesar. Even though this was exactly what the Jews were inclined to do anyway, they suddenly aligned themselves with the hated Romans in order to oppose the gospel of Jesus Christ.

We see the same in the world today. Any time we preach a radical Christianity—one that actually makes a difference in the lives of people—then we who keep the law of God are accused of being lawbreakers. Sometimes the issue is abortion, sometimes prayer in school, but the accusation always comes up.

In the same measure that you seriously intend to follow Jesus and his commandments, you are going to run into that kind of opposition. The issue boils down to this: Is Jesus Christ the King or not? Paul said he is, and if so, then his Lordship must rule over every part of our lives: physical, mental, spiritual, emotional, financial, and so on. It becomes an honor to be hated and accused by those who oppose Jesus.

Unfortunately, in our hearts we are such compromisers. We want to be popular even with those who hate our Master. We make concessions right and left with the ones who accuse our Lord, when instead we should count their hatred as evidence that we are following in Jesus' footsteps.

The Rewards of Confrontation

One of the most touching stories I've ever heard is about Aida Skripnikova, a Baptist girl from Leningrad. Aida accepted the Lord at age seventeen and was soon in trouble with the authorities. Again and again she was interrogated by the police, but she continued with her bold witness at every opportunity. She gave out gospel literature right in front of the atheist museum on the main thoroughfare of the city, and finally the authorities threw her into prison.

She was willing to pay the price, however. While in prison serving an incredibly difficult three-year sentence, Aida wrote a secret letter that was smuggled out. Among the gripping things it contained was this: "I've been told more than once that I can believe in God, but I'm to *act* as if I didn't. This is the condition on which freedom is offered to me more and more frequently. The devil has started saying to me, 'Don't reject God, just ignore his commands.' But to me, they mean the same thing."

As I read that letter, I could picture behind Aida the thousands of others in prisons and concentration camps who are paying the price because they boldly proclaim that Jesus Christ is King. Two other Baptist elders were arrested with Aida. One of them was told that he could live in Heaven according to the Bible, but not here on earth. He replied, "If I don't live according to the Bible on earth, I will never get to Heaven."

I believe he touched the very heart of the gospel here. The reward of godly confrontation is a clear witness for

Jesus Christ. So many Christians believe they can water down the message and live just the way they want, as long as they give the Lord his ten percent. Well, maybe they will get to Heaven through the grace of God, but at the very least they have wasted their lives on earth, never becoming the revolutionaries of love that God intends for us to be.

Paul wasn't like that. While still in the dust on the Damascus road, blinded by the light of God, he said immediately, "Lord, what do you want me to do?" And Jesus responded by telling him how much he would be privileged to suffer for the name of Jesus, at the same time supplying the necessary power to resist the enemy's onslaughts.

What a joyful reward to be able to stand up against the devil and win, no matter what the personal cost!

The Cost of Failing to Confront

Paul was aware that the cost of failing to confront the enemy is much higher than the personal price of standing against him. Remember the story of David and Goliath? The Philistines had invaded the territory of God's people, but the Israelites were unprepared to do battle. No weapons were to be found in Israel because the Philistines had commanded it. Talk about humiliation! The situation is similar today when atheistic governments try to tell God's people how many Bibles they can have. Are we going to let the enemy curtail our activities and prevent the church from winning the world, or will we obey Jesus and "make disciples of all nations" (Mt 28:19)?

When I read about the dedication of political revolutionaries today, I wonder how the church will ever defeat the enemy. You don't find communists worrying about giving a tithe to the party; they can't even be members without contributing 80% of their income. They're not concerned about friendship or marriage because they have freely given up everything for the revolution. Yet how many Christians will even give up Sunday night television for the sake of the gospel?

And who gets the ultimate blame for our failures? When Goliath stood on the hill God had given to his people, taunting the army of Israel, he was really despising the God of Israel. As Paul quoted from Isaiah, "The name of God is blasphemed . . . because of you" (Rom 2:24).

When we fail as Christians, we may be clever enough to escape responsibility, but our God will get the blame and ridicule. He gave the church the authority to win the world; if we fail, it reflects most of all on our Master.

As in all of Satan's dialogues, Goliath began with a lie. "Why have you come out in battle array?" he wanted to know. This was Israel's land, which had been invaded by the Philistines. The Israelites were only reclaiming what was rightfully theirs, yet Goliath acted as if they were intruding on *his* territory.

Any time we defend ourselves as believers, the enemy will pull out all stops and protest that we're fighting him unjustly. Yet we are only claiming our God-given rights: to have a Bible of our own . . . to give our children a Christian education . . . to protect the unborn. We have to stand our ground no matter what the enemy throws at us.

From the very first pages of the Bible, it has been clear that we are in a war. God himself declared holy war on the devil in Genesis 3. Of course, the devil is fighting back, attempting to destroy the plan God has already devised in Heaven.

Every evil done from creation to the coming of the Messiah was aimed at preventing Jesus from being born in Bethlehem. In response, God called people like you and me to be "heroes of the faith," to thwart the devil's plans, even at great personal cost.

The heroes of the Old Testament did their job and Jesus was born—the Lamb that was slain before the foundation of the world. God had already taken care of the problem of sin; all that was needed was the right *time* to fulfill the plan and the right *people* to carry out his purpose. Will we continue to be faithful to that purpose?

Wars are not won simply because one side is right; they are usually won by the people who are willing to pay the greater price for victory. Are we willing to proclaim the truth of the gospel, even when it means a confrontation? Are we willing to pay the ultimate price to see the gospel of Jesus Christ triumph in the world?

NINE

Jesus:
The Ultimate Hero

I REMEMBER HEARING A STORY about an English preacher and his son. The story was said to be authentic and went as follows:

Every Sunday morning the preacher and his son would come faithfully to their little church, even though the boy was sometimes the only congregation. At the entrance was an offering box, and as they went in, the father would put his coins in. Then the two of them would go through the service. Maybe somebody else would show up, maybe not. But no one else ever put money in the offering box. After the service, the father would empty the box and take out the money which was always exactly the same amount that he had put in.

One day the boy got a bright idea. "Daddy," he said, "if you put more into it, wouldn't you get more out of it?"

"Quite so," said his father. "Quite so, but it is not always easy."

Some of us may find it difficult to put more into our faith than is comfortable. Perhaps we do our duty faithfully, but find it risky to extend ourselves beyond familiar limits. We may choose to model our life after a familiar biblical hero or a contemporary Christian leader. We try to imitate them, and that's good. Even the apostle

Paul said, "Be imitators of me, as I am of Christ" (1 Cor 11:1). However, Paul's challenge to us was not merely to be like him; Paul always pointed to the ultimate model, Jesus Christ.

Those who have gone before us can assist us in following Christ, but we must reach beyond their example. Jesus Christ must be our greatest hero. We must follow him, imitate him, obey him. We must love him with all our heart, mind, and strength. Everything we have, everything we are, everything we ever will have or be must be his.

Of all the heroes that you may study, from the Old or New Testament, from church history or modern times—and I know some great ones today—there is none greater than Jesus himself. *Christian heroism is nothing short of being like Christ in every way.*

The first chapter of the Gospel of Mark gives us some important clues to what being like Jesus will mean.

The Discipline of Preparation

I must confess that I don't get up every morning of the year eager to do the will of God whatever the cost. I sometimes have to struggle on my knees with the Word in prayer and confession. But Jesus provides me with an inspiring model of preparation.

Prayer in the Morning

Mark 1:35 says, "And in the morning, a great while before day, he rose and went out to a lonely place, and there he prayed." Notice five things about Jesus' preparation to do God's will:

1. In the morning. For most of us, the most comfortable part of our day is early morning when we are resting in our warm beds. Naturally, we prefer to sleep in, but eventually, reluctantly, we get up. Some of us pick up a newspaper, or turn on the TV to catch "The Today Show." After a shower and getting dressed, we hurry off to work. At the end of the day we realize we have had no time for prayer. "God will understand our busyness," we reason. But Jesus himself made a point to *begin* the day in prayer.

2. A great while before day. Hudson Taylor, who for decades worked in China as a missionary, wrote some words at the end of his life that always challenge me: "As long as I was in China, the sun never rose without finding me on my knees." What a testimony! He took his cue from Jesus.

3. He rose. Don't try to pray in bed. You'll never make it. It will ruin your prayer, and it will ruin your rest.

4. He went out to a lonely place. Why did Jesus choose to get away? Because he had no home of his own, he was always a guest in someone else's home. In order to be undisturbed, he had to go out among the trees and hills. Most of us will also need to find a quiet place, away from the phone and other distractions.

5. There he prayed. He had work to do, and real prayer is real work, the prelude to all that God asks us to do.

This was the price of preparation that Jesus paid. If we are not willing to pay the price, then we're not going to get much out of our faith walk. Unless we're willing to put more in, we won't get more out. We have to wake up, get out, and get down on our knees.

The first year of my ministry, over thirty years ago, God told me: "Awake, and strengthen what remains and is on the point of death" (Rv 3:2). It became a commission to me. I had to live it; but first I had to wake up. But when I awoke, I began to see things the sleepers never saw. God began to reveal things to me early in the morning. The mind is fresh, the heart is empty, and the spirit is receptive to the voice of God. How important to start our day with God!

Prayer at Night

Prayer requires sacrifice. It is much easier to sleep, especially when you feel tired. When I read the life of Jesus, I'm sure he must have always been tired: the power that went out of him, the hours he spent teaching the disciples, all that walking throughout the land, the thousands of people who came to be ministered to, talked to, prayed for, fed, touched. But he never neglected his spiritual health.

Late in the evening after a full day of ministry when everyone was so tired that they "went each to his own house, . . . Jesus went to the Mount of Olives" (Jn 8:1). Another time Luke reported that at night when everyone else was very sleepy, Jesus went to the Mount of Olives to pray "as was his custom" (Lk 22:39).

How could he do it? Where did he get the power? Maybe that's the wrong question. We think of the power and stamina required to pray, but maybe it was the other way around: prayer was where he got his power for all other ministry. Jesus demonstrated that even the Son of God could not minister the way God wanted him to unless he took time to be alone with his heavenly Father.

Prayer Alone

Alone. That means when no one else is there. Alone is where our character is revealed. When we're in the limelight or on the podium or in front of the television camera, anyone—even me—can be a spiritual actor. But when I'm alone in the dark, only God sees me. That's where I become a man of God.

But alone with God is where I catch a glimpse of his vision for the world. If I do not wake up, get out, and get on my knees, I will never see what others do not see. God wants us to be visionaries who are acquainted with the need in the world from his point of view. It takes effort, but the more we put into our time alone with God, the more we will get out of it.

We all want to cuddle up to other people. We think that we always need fellowship, so we never get alone. But we may miss God's best for our life because we're not really following Jesus; we're just staying close to other people. Let's make sure that we do more praying in secret, in a lonely place, and the results will be visible, tangible, full of power.

The Foundation of Character

After Jesus got up early and went out to pray, Mark's Gospel says, "Simon and those who were with him pursued him, and they found him and said to him, 'Everyone is searching for you.'" (Mk 1:36, 37). Has anyone ever sought you out? Have they ever made a journey to see you because of your character?

You don't become an elder or leader in the church just because someone appoints you to that position. You are an elder because people come to you with their problems. As your personal ministry develops, you may be appointed in a formal way—that's the way it is supposed to work. The appointment does not make you an elder. Your personal life, your character, the way you use your spiritual gifts make you an elder or counselor or older brother or sister to others who are in need of God's love.

The raising of Lazarus from the dead (cf. John 11)

displayed the tremendous power Jesus had. In the next chapter, a great crowd came to see Lazarus, and Scripture says, "So the chief priests planned to put Lazarus also to death, because on account of him many of the Jews were going away and believing in Jesus" (Jn 12:10, 11). When God does a great work in us, many other people will believe. That's the power that comes out of a changed character. Godly power is a very personal thing which comes from following Jesus Christ very closely.

Motivated by a Mission

When the disciples came searching for Jesus, " . . . he said to them, 'Let us go on to the next towns, that I may preach there also; for that is why I came out.' And he went throughout all Galilee, preaching in their synagogues and casting out demons" (Mk 1:28, 39). When Jesus went out, it was always with a mission. He knew what he was doing. What a difference it makes when we know that we have been sent for a purpose.

Jesus went to the synagogues throughout all Galilee, preaching and casting out the demons. Preaching is always a matter of aggressive evangelism. You don't wait until someone comes to you to begin preaching. Today we usually build big churches and expect people to come to us. But that is not the New Testament way. Jesus went out to where the people were. A fisherman should go out with his net to where the fish are. Don't put a beautiful net up on the beach, then sing songs and expect the fish to jump out of the sea into the net. We must go to them.

Moved with Compassion

As Jesus moved out among the people, " . . . a leper came to him beseeching him, and kneeling said to him, 'If you will, you can make me clean.' Moved with pity, he stretched out his hand and touched him, and said to him, 'I will; be clean'" (Mk 1:40, 41). Do you know what compassion is? Compassion is love that feels another's pain. We need another dimension to our love; we need to love where it hurts. Among all the people pressing around to see him, Jesus saw the lepers and those possessed by demons. He sees all sick people, oppressed people, people in need or afraid.

What made Jesus reach out to the leper? What made him cast out demons? It was the love of God living in him. Of Jesus it is said that "in Him dwells all the fullness of the Godhead bodily" (Col 2:9 NKJV). Jesus' whole nature was so filled with the presence of God that he simply could not tolerate evil and suffering. But there is nothing that Jesus had that we cannot have. We, too, can have the fullness of the Spirit. We can have the love of God which reaches out, enabling us to go beyond our own limitations.

Guided by Righteousness

The character of Jesus is also described by Paul as he quoted the psalmist: "[The Son] hast loved righteousness and hated lawlessness" (Heb 1:9). Jesus hated not only sin but also every result of sin. We may not always be able to analyze and diagnose sin, but we can always see the results: children torn between divorced parents; Christian leaders pointing fingers at each other and tearing each other down; people's lives ruined by drugs or alcohol; air pollution; animals at the edge of extinction; whole groups of people denied basic rights; nations poised for war; the church persecuted all over the globe.

But righteousness does not just see; it acts. Demons at work? Jesus came with deliverance. Illness? He came with healing. Sin? He brought the gospel. Death? He brought life. Rebellion? He brought reconciliation. Injustice and lawlessness? He came with the principles of God. These are the solutions that we have to offer to the world today.

As Christians, we must especially care for the suffering church; we cannot expect earthly governments to provide real protection. Remember: the battle is a spiritual one. Governments can't bring real solutions. That's what we are equipped to do.

We must never allow evil to continue to take away the basic rights of the people. Everyone has the right to hear who Jesus is, the right to worship God, the right to own a Bible, believe the Bible, preach the Bible, and live the Bible.

The Results of Action

In Mark 1 we discover that Jesus' preparation and character resulted in the leper's healing: "And immediately the leprosy left him, and he was made clean" (Mk 1:42). There was a complete change.

People Will Be Changed

In order to become real heroes of the faith, we must ask ourselves whether we really believe people can be changed by Jesus. Every encounter with Jesus caused a change in people: the weak became strong; the sick were healed; the despondent received courage; captives received liberty; the broken were made whole. But do we really believe that is true? Are we unashamedly evangelical in our view? If not, we cannot be heroes of the faith.

The World Will Get What It Needs

Freedom is a biblically-based ideal, and the liberty to worship God is an especially God-given right. However, I don't think the Bible indicates a clear preference for any specific political or economic system. Therefore I don't think it is the Christian's primary purpose to work for or against any earthly political or economic system— capitalist, communist, colonial, or monarchy. That's not what the world really needs.

In fact, if the church in China or Russia grows more under persecution than it was ever able to grow when the missionaries could freely operate, then why should I resist that system, *per se*? Our business is to be *for* the advancement of the Kingdom of God, not *against* this or that form of worldly government. If I am for Jesus and his righteousness, then there will obviously be conflicts with evil. I will resist every principle of unrighteousness and cross any border to share the gospel. But that's different than directly advocating one form of government and opposing another. The conflicts come because of the gospel, not because of a political agenda.

Some people say you can't preach the gospel in one country, and you can't tell children about Jesus in another country. Nonsense. You might get arrested like Peter and Paul and Jesus did, but *you can still do it if you will.* They never let such threats stop them, and neither have many believers who have endured persecution throughout the ages.

The Gospel Will Be Made Known

Recently our Open Doors Asia correspondent, Ron MacMillan, reported that the government of China may be tightening its controls again on the church ("Christians in Central China Issued New Prohibitions Curtailing Church Activities," *Open Doors News Service,* Aug. 10, 1987, pp. 8, 9). For instance, Public Security officials recently intercepted a letter written by a prominent evangelist to two new converts in central China. The letter contained advice suitable for new Christians and included a quote from the Bible, which said, "The Lord is righteous, gracious, and full of love."

The converts were picked up and interrogated for eight hours and then presented with a list of five prohibitions severely limiting their religious activity. The list prohibits them from (1) witnessing to anyone about Christ—a right granted only to pastors registered in the Three-Self Patriotic Movement, (2) baptizing anyone—unless they have permission from the local Three-Self pastor, (3) attending a house church meeting, (4) listening to any Christian broadcasts, and (5) accepting any imported Bibles or Christian literature. The officials were unusually uncompromising in their warning, stressing that these were not just guidelines but the "laws of the land to be vigorously upheld."

Only a few months before, a group of six members of the "Jesus Family," the largest Christian group in the northern provinces of China, was arrested, tied up, suspended from branches, and brutally beaten by guards in an attempt to force them to leave their local fellowship. (Ron MacMillan, "'Jesus Family' Leaders Arrested in Crackdown Against Chinese Pentecostals," *Open Doors News Service,* July 8, 1987, p. 3.)

And yet, in spite of persecution, the church in China has been growing at a remarkable rate. When China became communist in 1949, there were only about 700,000 Protestant believers after 100 years of missionary effort. Now many observers estimate the number of believers at over 50 million.

What happened after Jesus healed the leper shows just how unrestrainable the gospel is. Even when Jesus wanted to temporarily keep it quiet, he couldn't.

And he [Jesus] sternly charged him, and sent him away at once, and said to him, "See that you say nothing to any one; but go, show yourself to the priest, and offer for your cleansing what Moses commanded, for a proof to the people." But he went out and began to talk freely about it, and to spread the news, so that Jesus could no longer openly enter a town, but was out in the country; and people came to him from every quarter.

(Mk 1:43-45)

Those who truly live a Christ-like life are absolutely the most attractive people in the world. The One we emulate attracted people of all ages, from all walks of life. Jesus spent time with children and with adults. He's *the* hero of the faith.

When Jesus returned to the Father, he commissioned his disciples—both present and future—to proclaim the salvation he had finished on the cross, and to continue the work he had begun in the power of the Holy Spirit. When we decide that we will only follow him, walk as he walked, love as he loved, and do as he did, then things will happen in our lives that happened in his life, every day, every hour, every minute.

TEN

How You Can
Be a Hero of the Faith

D O YOU KNOW WHAT *JIHAD* IS? This expression is found in the Koran, and is what Iran's Ayatollah Khomeini has waged on his neighbors in Iraq and other Arab countries. Many Arab countries would like to do this to Israel. *Jihad* is a "holy war": total, all-out war.

The amazing thing is that God himself has declared *jihad.* In Genesis 3:15 he issued the challenge to Satan: "I will put enmity between you and the woman, / and between your seed and her seed; / he shall bruise your head, / and you shall bruise his heel." God has declared total war against everything that stands in opposition to his holiness, his righteousness, his justice, and his love. As far as he is concerned there can never be any compromise between good and evil. God is not very diplomatic in this regard. God is a warrior, and he calls his people to spiritual battle.

Spiritual warfare is raging all around us today. It's not just the house churches meeting illegally in China, or Christians who are forbidden to proselytize in Muslim countries, who know its reality. In fact, it's sometimes easier to stand firm and fight when war has been openly declared! But all of us face this battle from every side. We see it in the seductive and popular appeal of the New Age Movement; in the way "responsible sex" (i.e., using contraceptives) has replaced sexual purity; in the way abortion and euthanasia have been "re-phrased" to sound acceptable and compassionate; in the way "personal fulfillment" is replacing "commitment" as a priority in marriage; in the way "freedom of religion" is coming to mean "freedom *from* religion"; in the way materialism and self-interest has numbed our sensitivity to those who suffer around the world—and in our own backyard; in the way drug traffickers are leaving a trail of ruined young lives for personal profit; in the way we put our trust in a nuclear arsenal.

A battle needs heroes who are willing to put their lives on the line, and spiritual warfare needs heroes of the faith willing to do the same.

That is what this book is about. The people in the Bible whom we've called heroes of the faith—all those men and women of God who were used so mightily by him—were people engaged in spiritual warfare. These biblical heroes seem larger than life to us today—Moses, the great emancipator! David, the king after God's own heart!—yet in their time, they were just ordinary people who were willing to stand up for the truth of God, speak the truth, and act on it. And that is what we are called to do today.

But to fight this battle, we need to be equipped. We must *know* God's Word, we must *live* God's Word, we must *speak* God's Word, we must put God's Word into the hands of all peoples.

Equipping the Heroes of the Faith

Anyone who stands up and boldly proclaims the Word of God today will not only have a following but, in most cases, opposition as well. That is why the need is greater than ever for people to be trained in the Word of God. In Ephesians 6:10-17, Paul the warrior describes how God equips us for battle:

> Finally, be strong in the Lord and in the strength of his might. Put on the whole armor of God, that you may be able to stand against the wiles of the devil. For we are not contending against flesh and blood, but against the principalities, against the powers, against the world rulers of this present darkness, against the spiritual hosts of wickedness in the heavenly places. Therefore take the whole armor of God, that you may be able to withstand in the evil day, and having done all, to stand. Stand therefore, having girded your loins with truth, and having put on the breastplate of righteousness, and having shod your feet with the equipment of the gospel of peace; besides all these, taking the shield of faith, with which you can quench all the flaming darts of the evil one. And take the helmet of salvation and the sword of the Spirit, which is the word of God.

No Provision for Retreat

It is important to note that in all this equipment there is no protection for our backs. God has not equipped us to run away from conflict. This reveals much about God's whole approach and the role he expects us to fulfill. If our objective were to avoid conflict with the enemy, we would never win the battle. Instead, we are to be warriors, aggressively and offensively facing the enemy, not trying to escape.

A famous Czech communist once said, "I can only honor my opponent in a debate if he makes an all-out effort to convert me." But because so few Christians are willing to stand up and openly challenge the communist philosophy with the Word of God, they despise us. We do not win our opponent by refusing to debate him, but by openly confronting falsehood with truth.

This is one reason we Christians in the free world must help provide what every suffering Christian in the world needs most—a copy of the Bible. It is our mission at Open Doors to give the suffering church the weapon it needs to wage spiritual warfare.

Only One Weapon

Paul tells us to take up the "sword of the Spirit, which is the Word of God." All the other parts of the spiritual armor are defensive. The sword is offensive. By it we make forward progress in defeating the enemy.

The weapons God has provided for the Christian to use are not bombs and guns, not economic leverage and boycotts, not even education or diplomatic negotiations. This is because, as Paul says, "we are not contending against flesh and blood, but against the principalities, against the powers, against the world rulers of this present darkness, against the spiritual hosts of wickedness in the heavenly places." Those evil forces do create tangible earthly suffering and oppression, but *the* weapon God has empowered us to use is the Sword of the Spirit, which is the Word of God.

Quenching Satan's Darts

The devil also uses weapons. To be effective warriors we must know our enemy and understand the kinds of weapons he uses. The devil's main weapon is to sow doubt in our trust of the Word of God. The first time he employed this weapon was in the Garden of Eden. He opened with a challenge: "Did God say . . . ?" (Gn 3:1). If he can disable our only weapon by questioning its reliability, he gains a great advantage in undoing any hero of the faith.

The devil will try that tactic with anyone. He even tried it with Jesus. When he knew that Jesus was weak after fasting and praying in the desert for forty days and forty nights, then Satan came and tried to make him doubt the reliability of the Word of God.

The greatest weakness in our churches today is the lack of assurance. We do not know what we should know. We do not know our God. We do not know the power of the blood of Jesus. We do not know how to quote the Scripture. We do not know how to wield the Sword of the Spirit. When Jesus was tempted, his every defense was the Word of God: "It is written. . . ," he countered.

Anytime we try to argue with the devil on any other basis than what is written in the Word of God, we are sure to lose. The devil has had thousands of years of experience with people, plenty of time to think up a confounding answer to any smart remark we might devise. We have only one effective weapon and that is the Word of God. Only that will make us heroes of the faith.

Walking in the Path God Has Chosen for You

There is another lesson that can be learned from Jesus' struggle with the devil in the wilderness. Satan challenged Jesus to prove that he was the Son of God by leaping off the pinnacle of the temple. This challenge was based on Psalm 91:11-12 which promised that the angels would protect him. Sounds good, doesn't it? A sure way for Jesus to prove that he was the Son of God. And yet the context of Psalm 91 includes an important qualification. The person of whom the psalmist spoke walked in the way of God in three important areas:

He was in the right place. Verse 1 speaks of the one "who

dwells in the shelter of the Most High, / who abides in the shadow of the Almighty."

He was doing the right thing. Verse 9 says the protection is "because you have made the Lord your refuge, the Most High your habitation."

He was in the right relationship. Verse 14 commends the fact that he "cleaves to me in love."

Satan actually left out one little phrase right in the middle of the Scripture he quoted. The verse said that the angels will guard him "in all your ways [or paths]." Satan left that out. Maybe he didn't want to remind Jesus that the only paths with God's protection are the paths of God's will.

Why are so many Christians weak and ineffective? With all of the accumulated knowledge we have of the Scriptures and church history and counseling and psychology and psychiatry and everything else, many are still trying to be heroes along paths God has not led them.

If God calls you to become a warrior, become a warrior. If God calls you to become an intercessor, become an intercessor. If God calls you to be a Bible smuggler with Open Doors, become a Bible smuggler with Open Doors. But if God calls you to raise a family for him, or be his witness in the marketplace, don't try to do something else.

I remember when I was a very young Christian, my first desire was to be a missionary. I went to an old pastor in Holland and I said, "Pastor, I want to go to the mission field."

I thought he would pat me on the shoulder and say, "Good boy, Andrew." But no. With a very serious face he said, "Well, Andrew, maybe that is the only place where God can keep you from backsliding." I didn't like that message because it didn't seem to reflect a very high opinion of me. But the older I grew the more I came to agree with him. The question is, are you in the right *way?*—the way God has chosen for *you?*

God has a *way* for each one of us where we can become a warrior for God, and that is the only place where God can protect you. If Jesus had followed Satan's suggestion when he misquoted Scripture, if Jesus had jumped, I believe he might have lost his life and would never have gone to the cross that he came to embrace.

Dangers to Avoid

The son of a friend of mine is very interested in medieval history. He likes to dress up like a knight and, using wooden swords and shields, have mock battles with his friends. More than once he's come in from the back yard with a scrape or bruise from a whack with a wooden sword.

But real swords present real dangers—just like any modern weapon. A person who uses a weapon to hunt or for self-defense or in the army can be infinitely more hazardous to himself or others if he is not aware of the dangers to avoid. This is true of the Sword of the Spirit, as well.

Misuse of Scripture

The experience in the Garden of Eden referred to earlier is instructive in another way. Not only did Satan introduce doubt about the reliability of God's word, but Eve made a mistake in the way she handled God's word. She misquoted God. God had said, "You may freely eat of every tree of the garden; but of the tree of the knowledge of good and evil you shall not eat, for in the day that you eat of it you shall die" (Gn 2:16, 17). However, when Eve quoted God's words, she added a little: "You shall not eat of the fruit of the tree which is in the midst of the garden, *neither shall you touch it*, lest you die" (Gn 3:3, emphasis added).

It's just as dangerous to add to the Word of God as it is to take away from it. In this case, there is no record of God telling Adam and Eve not to touch the tree, so when Satan responded, "You will not die," he had the strategic advantage of a half truth. Indeed, when Eve touched the tree she didn't die, so, she reasoned, why not go ahead and eat the fruit?

How many people have been turned away from the gospel when they encountered a commandment of man being preached as the Word of God? By one means or another, people always discover that the commandments of men are not true and just, and when they do, they think their discovery gives them justification to dismiss the whole gospel.

Eve may have had an excuse for misquoting God. His commandments were not yet written down. But we have no such excuse. We can turn to the Bible and see exactly what he has said or didn't say. Therefore, we have a great responsibility to handle the Word of God properly. Think of the consequences of that first mishandling of God's Word—the whole human race fell into sin!

Satan's Misuse of Scripture

As we noted earlier in the instance of Jesus's temptation in the wilderness, the devil can also quote the Word. But be careful when people who are not true believers start quoting Scripture. You may be asking, "How am I supposed to know who to trust when so many people back up their views with Scripture and yet hold such different opinions on things?"

I cannot offer a solution for resolving all the debates among genuine Christians. But we would be far ahead if we would discern that some of the turmoil comes from decidedly non-Christian sources, even though they may quote the Bible. The apostle John said: "Beloved, do not believe every spirit, but test the spirits to see whether they are of God; for many false prophets have gone out into the world. By this you know the Spirit of God: every spirit which confesses that Jesus Christ has come in the flesh is of God" (1 Jn 4:1, 2). To consistently apply that basic litmus test would remove a lot of confusion.

For instance, when Jesus responded with the Word of God during his temptation in the wilderness by saying, "It is written...," Satan tried quoting Scripture, too. But from the moment he opened his mouth, the devil disqualified himself according to John's test. Satan's first words questioned Jesus' divinity: "*If* you are the Son of God..." (Mt 4:3). Anyone who does not clearly confess that Jesus is the Christ, the only begotten Son of the living God, is suspect from the outset in terms of what they might teach us regarding matters of faith. No matter how innocent, educated, or religious, they unknowingly may be the mouthpiece of a much more sinister force.

Trying to Go It Alone

As we accept God's call to become a hero of the faith, a fighter for the Lord, each of us may wonder how we can develop the confidence to face the enemy single-handedly. In a world full of hatred, rampant sin, and evil ideologies, can you go in alone and establish a work for God?

Let's first establish that going it alone is not the ideal way. God has called us into a fellowship—church congregations and ministries—and together we are part of the army of the Lord. That is why God gives different gifts to different people, so that we can work together to build up the Kingdom of God. It is as Christ's Body that we should move out into the world and win the world for Christ, not as individual Lone Rangers.

However, I believe it is possible to stand alone for Christ. Throughout the Scriptures we see many men and women who had to stand alone in order to accomplish something important for God by faith—just read Hebrews 11. We need to know that we *can* because there will be times when we have to stand alone—or at least it may feel that way, as it did to Elijah, even when there were still seven thousand in Israel who had not bowed their knee to Baal (1 Kgs 19:18). We may feel like the only parents who won't let their son or daughter stay out all night—stand firm! You may feel like the only guy at work that doesn't tell dirty jokes—stand firm! You may be the only member of your family willing to give up an impressive salary to serve the poor at home or overseas—stand firm!

We need to know that God has equipped us through his Spirit and with his Word to be fully capable soldiers, fit for any combat into which he sends us. Without that confidence, our nerve won't be steady under fire. We'll be looking to the right and the left for help from others when we should be facing the enemy head on.

Where You Can Enter the Battle

Not only has God declared *jihad,* so has the devil. In Revelation we find something very interesting: "These are of one mind and give over their power and authority to the beast; they will make war on the Lamb, and the Lamb will conquer them, for he is Lord of lords and King of kings, and those with him are called and chosen and faithful" (Rv 17:13, 14).

Jihad originated with God, but all the enemies of Christ temporarily unite together to make war on the Lamb. They may hate each other, but their common hatred for the Lamb is greater than their hatred of each other, so together they declare *jihad* on the Lamb.

Be a Worthy Target

Notice that this passage in Revelation does not say that they will make war on the church as an organization. Even today there are hostile places in the world where some expressions of the church are not really persecuted. If you compromise enough, let the state regulate your activities, don't evangelize or make any waves, then there is the possibility of continuing to function without much persecution.

It's not even the individual believer who is automatically the target of persecution. One may be a nominal Christian and get along quite well with a very evil system. Take, for example, many so-called Christians under Hitler and the Nazis. They kept their mouths shut, they closed their eyes, and they were not persecuted. But what happened to the "confessing church?" It had to go underground, just as Corrie ten Boom and her family went underground in their attempts to shelter the Jews in obedience to Christ.

The Lamb of God is Satan's ultimate target. And it's the life of Christ in the believer and in the church—*Christ in you*—that is the target of persecution.

Unfortunately, some Christians unwittingly play right into Satan's battle scheme, like a basketball player that sinks a shot into the opponent's basket. When "big name" Christians fight and quarrel with each other over public airwaves, the Lamb of God is wounded. When a church ignores its needy neighbors, it is Christ that is ignored. When Christian organizations mismanage their funds, Christ's name is defiled. When Christians drag other Christians into court, it is Christ that is judged.

I'm so glad the battle doesn't stop there. I'm glad we

can know the end of the story, because the Lamb does overcome. Scripture doesn't say that the enemy will break his teeth when he tries to chew on a passive Lamb. No. The Lamb will also fight! There is a spiritual war going on in which every individual Christian is invited to take part. And we can fight in confidence because we know who wins! The Lamb overcomes because he is Lord of lords and King of kings, and those who are with him are the called and chosen and faithful.

This, then, is the message that we have for the suffering church worldwide: "If you are persecuted, rejoice! It is just about the surest proof that the Son of God lives in you; otherwise you wouldn't be persecuted. Take courage, go back to the Word of God." As we share God's Word and study it together, we will begin to understand that from the first declaration of *jihad* in Genesis 3:15 to the declaration of *jihad* by the devil in Revelation 17:13, the whole book is one record of warfare, conflict, and spiritual battle—fought by heroes of the faith. They are not heroes because they were born with some superior power; they became heroes because they yielded their lives to Jesus Christ. Taking the risk, they said, "Lord, your will be done in my life."

Be Urgent to Spread the Word

Most problems in the world are not political issues but spiritual. It's a battle for the minds and hearts of men and women. The enemy lies, intimidates, misquotes Scripture, or invents a new religion with a different "holy book." The only answer is to rightly handle the Word of Truth which can make people free as individuals, and make nations free.

People need to know what the Scriptures say, but to do this they must have access to the Word of God for study and meditation. That's why it is so important to make the

Word of God available to every nation in the world. No military assistance, no diplomatic power, no economic aid or food we give to any nation is going to make a basic difference in the world situation because it does not change the attitude of people toward life, toward sin, toward the devil, and toward God. As Peter said, "Lord, to whom shall we go? You have the words of eternal life" (Jn 6:68). And that is true for the whole world; only Jesus as revealed in the Word of God can bring real life. That's why I have dedicated my life to spreading the Word of God as the only solution to man's deepest problems, even when I talk about politics.

Horace Greeley, the famous American communicator and leader in the antislavery movement during the last century, made a marvelous statement: "It is impossible to enslave mentally or socially a Bible-reading people." The principles of the Bible are the groundwork of human freedom. If we make the Word of God available, no evil ideology, no strange philosophy, no idolatrous religion can effectively take hold of any people in a permanent way. The Bible is the only book that does not need a defense; it has stood the test for centuries; it continues to change lives. It has the words of eternal life.

Exodus 15 records the Song of Moses, and in it is the line: "The Lord is a man of war; / the Lord is his name" (Ex 15:3). Interestingly, when we go to the end of the Bible, we find in Revelation 15:3 that the conquering saints are still singing the Song of Moses. Throughout this entire age, until evil has been completely banished, the Lord is identified as a man of war, standing in the gap, calling people to follow his example and do likewise.

Brothers and sisters, the time is now. The battle is all around us; are you feeling afraid? Look up—Christ goes before you, accompanied by many heroes of the faith who have gone before. Learn from their example. Pick up the Sword of the Spirit, learn to use it well, bring its light into the dark places, strike down falsehood with truth. Let us heed God's call to become heroes of the faith, so that we can say with the apostle Paul, "I have fought the good fight, I have finished the race, I have kept the faith" (2 Tm 4:7).

Open Doors News Brief
(U.S. and Canada Only)

If you would like to know more about Open Doors with Brother Andrew and its ministry to the Suffering Church, write to the address below. We'll send you a free six-month subscription to the *Open Doors News Brief.* This monthly publication will bring you timely news and information about persecuted Christians around the world.

Open Doors with Brother Andrew

P.O. Box 27001	P.O. Box 597
Santa Anna, CA 92799	Streetsville, ON L5M 2C1
United States	**Canada**

If you live outside the U.S. or Canada and would like more information, write the Open Doors office nearest you:

Australia
P.O. Box 53—Seaforth, NSW—Australia 2092

England
P.O. Box 6—Standlake, Witney—
Oxon OX8 7SP—England

The Netherlands
P.O. Box 47—3850AA Ermelo—The Netherlands

New Zealand
P.O. Box 6123—Auckland 1—New Zealand

Singapore
1 Sophia Road—#03-28, Peace Centre—
Singapore 0922

South Africa
P.O. Box 990099—Kibler Park—
2053 Johannesburg—S. Africa